Taking the Cross of Christ to the Campus

A Manual for Church-Based Campus Ministry

William J. Senn III

BOB JONES
UNIVERSITY PRESS

Greenville, South Carolina

Library of Congress Cataloging-in-Publication Data

Senn, William J., 1958–

Taking the cross of Christ to the campus : a manual for church-based campus ministry / William J. Senn III.

p. cm.

Summary: "This book is a manual for church-based ministry to the college campus"—Provided by publisher.

Includes bibliographical references.

ISBN 978-1-59166-810-7 (perfect bound pbk. : alk. paper)

1. Church work with young adults. 2. Church work with students. I. Title.

BV4446.S46 2008

259'.24—dc22

2007036243

Cover Photo Credits: iStockphoto Inc.

All Scripture is quoted from the Authorized King James Version unless otherwise noted.

Taking the Cross of Christ to the Campus: A Manual for Church-Based Campus Ministry

William J. Senn III

Design by Nathan Hutcheon

Page layout by Michael Boone

© 2008 BJU Press

Greenville, South Carolina 29614

Bob Jones University Press is a division of BJU Press

Printed in the United States of America

ISBN 978-1-59166-810-7

15 14 13 12 11 10 9 8 7 6 5 4 3 2 1

Taking the Cross of Christ to the Campus
is dedicated to my wife, Allissa.
"Thou art all fair, my love; there is no
spot in thee." (Song of Sol. 4:7)

CONTENTS

ACKNOWLEDGMENTS

I would like to express my appreciation and love for the three women in my life: my wife Allissa, "the fairest among women," who has been my faithful helpmate for twenty-five years; my Episcopal-Baptist mother, Allison C. Rice; and my favorite mother-in-law, Aileen Isbell. I would like to also express my appreciation for the three boys in my life, John, Jim, and Ben. Thanks for all your support when dad has been so busy.

I would like to express my appreciation for the three churches in my life: Mt. Calvary Church of Elizabethtown for their support in my seminary training, and special thanks for the church families of University Baptist Church in Clemson, South Carolina, and Tri-City Baptist Church in Westminster, Colorado, which have invested and sacrificed so this manual on campus ministry could be completed.

I would like to express my appreciation for the three editors in my life: Kami Fitch, Peter Landry, and Mary Vose. I would like to express my appreciation for the three men who have been of great help on this project: Dr. Ward Andersen, Dr. Steve Hankins, and Dr. Dan Olinger.

Above all, I would like to express my gratitude to the great Three in One.

1

INTRODUCTION

NEED FOR STUDY

One of the most neglected ministries for the local church is an outreach to the secular college campus. This manual confronts this problem and presents a plan of attack for the local church to organize a campus ministry that is based squarely on the Great Commission. Consequently, this manual is simply an application of the Great Commission: to evangelize and disciple the fifteen million students enrolled in America's universities and colleges.

Historically, the fundamentalist movement has never solidly approached the secular campus from a strong local-church base. The ministries that have thrived on the secular campus have been the parachurch variety. Unfortunately, due to the lack of accountability with a local church and a weak view of the doctrine of biblical separation, they have become "religion gone free enterprise."[1]

Organizations such as InterVarsity, Campus Crusade and the Navigators were once supported, endorsed, equipped, and staffed by the fundamentalist movement.[2] Sadly, such organizations have

---

[1]Charles Dunn, *Campus Crusade: Its Message and Methods* (Greenville, SC: Bob Jones University Press, 1981), 19. What makes this quotation more significant is that Dr. Dunn is quoting from the new evangelical editor of *Eternity Magazine*.

[2]In 1950, Dawson Trotman was looking for "top notchers" for his ministry, the Navigators. That year he recruited over four hundred students from Bob Jones University (Betty Lee Skinner, *DAWS* [Grand Rapids: Zondervan, 1974], 312). Likewise, Bill Bright and Campus Crusade recruited workers from Bob Jones University until Bright compromised with ecumenical evangelist Dr. Billy Graham at the San Francisco Crusade in the late 1950s. When Bright made his decision to work with Graham, ten members of his staff, all Bob Jones graduates,

crossed over into new evangelicalism and ecumenical evangelism and are now heading back to Rome.[3] Over the past sixty years, the fundamentalist movement has gradually turned the secular campuses over to the new evangelicals, the liberals, the cults, the Muslims, and other groups. One illustration of this trend is that today there are less than fifty fundamental campus missionaries on our secular campuses. This manual is written to challenge and equip the fundamental local church in a college town to strive to have a campus presence for the Lord Jesus Christ.

PREVIOUS STUDIES

Most efforts to reach the secular campus have been divorced from the local church. This manual argues that the best model for reaching the secular campus is via a local church that is burdened for reaching collegians for Christ and that has the backing of other fundamental churches in the same state or region. The manual

---

quit on the spot (Charles Woodbridge, *Campus Crusade: Examined in the Light of Scripture* [Greenville, SC: Bob Jones University Press, 1970], 30).

[3]InterVarsity is dedicated to ecumenical relationships with the Roman Catholic Church and has stated that they will no longer tell Catholics that the idolatry their church teaches will take them to hell (*Eternity Magazine* [November, 1971]). InterVarsity Press has published books by Roman Catholics (e.g., *Handbooks of Christian Apologetics* [1994], written by two Catholic professors at the Catholic Boston College). On September 30, 1990, Bill Bright stated on the John Ankerberg Show that Campus Crusade had yoked together with 227 different Christian organizations, including the Roman Catholic Church, in showing the "JESUS" film. Bright defended hiring Roman Catholics for his Campus Crusade staff by stating that he could "work with anyone who calls Jesus Lord." Terry Taylor of the Navigators, James Dobson, Rabbi Howard Hirsch, and Catholic Bishop Richard C. Hanifena signed an agreement in April of 1993 called the *Covenant of Mutual Respect.* The intent of the covenant was for Christian leaders to agree not to evangelize Catholics and Jewish youth in Colorado Springs, Colorado. The document states, "The diversity of our religious perspectives may lead us into areas of possible disagreement. It is our hope to address those areas of difference with an attitude of openness, respect and love, and a willingness to listen and learn from each other to the end that we may manifest the ministry of reconciliation" (*The Catholic Herald* [June 2, 1993]). On September 14, 2000, at the Navigators' National Leadership Team meeting, Navigators affirmed "the legitimacy and strategic value of ministry with Catholics." Alan Andrews, a staff worker at the U.S. headquarters for the Navigators, states in this e-mail correspondence that "there is room to run in ministering with Catholics as Catholics. Catholic disciples can enrich the Navigator culture." Alan Andrews, e-mail to Navigators field staff, September 14, 2000.

instructs the local church on how to charter a campus organization as well as how to maintain and advance a campus ministry once it is chartered. Because the local church has historically been left out of campus ministry, this manual provides many original contributions in this area. Despite the many books, periodicals, pamphlets, and other publications referenced in the manual's selected bibliography, the author has found nothing that deals specifically with the local church hosting its own unique campus ministry. The closest writings on the subject are found in a handful of master of ministry projects. Daniel Duncan, a master's student at International School of Theology, wrote his master's project on *Community Colleges: Methodology for Developing Ongoing Campus Ministries*. This work demonstrates the need and the challenge of ministering to community college students. Duncan's contribution to this work is the heightened awareness of the large percentage of college students who are attending community colleges. Dennis Mitchel, a Dallas Theological Seminary student, wrote his master's research project on *A Disciple-Making Manual for the Secularized Campus*. This project emphasizes the theology of discipleship but is very limited in practical application to the secular campus. A similar work was written by Paul Bledsoe, a Cincinnati Christian Seminary student, entitled *Making Disciples of University Students*. Both of these master research projects emphasized the theology of discipleship but were very limited to its practical application on a secular campus. Mee L. Kong, a Calvary Theological Seminary student, wrote his master's project on *A Biblical Approach to Chinese Campus Ministry*. This work emphasizes small Bible study groups and discipleship with an aim to reach the Chinese college student. None of these works address the relationship of the local church with the campus ministry.

This lack of literature exposes the need for such a manual to be written. The majority of books written on campus ministry present the ministry through the eyes of the parachurch organization or the missionary model.[4] The local church is pictured as being

---

[4]Baptist Mid-Missions has a campus ministry division called Campus Bible Fellowship. They have printed a manual for their missionaries and participating churches that describes their philosophy of campus ministry and their relationship to the local church(es) in a college town. *Campus Bible Fellowship Staff Manual*

inadequate or uninterested in campus ministry. It is interesting to see what Charles H. Spurgeon said about the responsibility of the local church and missionary societies. In Spurgeon's sermon "The Church—Conservative and Aggressive," preached on May 19, 1861, he said,

> In order to spread the doctrines of the gospel, we have formed societies. There are missionary societies appended to every denomination. These societies are to be pillars and grounds of the truth, not so much in the maintenance of the truth as in the spreading of it. . . . We have been wondering why our societies have not greater success. I believe the reason is because there is not a single word in the Book of God about anything of the kind. The Church of God is the pillar and ground of the truth, not a society. The Church of God never ought to have delegated to any society whatever, a work which it behooved her to have done herself. Instead of sending our subscriptions to associations, we ought to have picked our own men out of our midst, and found the means to send them forth to preach the truth as it is in Jesus, ourselves. Now, do not misunderstand me. I would not say a single word against any society for the spread of God's truth. But I must repeat yet again, that all societies of that sort spring from an irregular and unscriptural position of the Church. The Church, if she were in her right state, would do the whole of the work herself. The city missionary would be a member of the Church, sent out and supported by the Church itself. The missionary to foreign lands would have the Church at his back, to whom he would look for support both in prayers and in subscriptions. I may be wrong, but this has deeply laid upon my soul; and I shall never be satisfied till I see in this Church an organization so complete that it does not need a supplement, able to do every good work, and fulfill every needful office of itself, and by itself, welcoming ever the cooperation of others, but never needing to

---

and the *Campus Bible Fellowship Area Liaison Committee Manual* are outstanding works and are some of the few manuals that even address the issue. The difference between Baptist Mid-Missions' manual and this manual is in the emphasis given to the local church and the model of campus pastor/missionary versus the traditional missionary model.

depend upon a society for the accomplishment of any purpose to which the Lord God hath been pleased to call it.[5]

Because there is so little information available that relates campus ministry to the local church, the majority of this manual then is the result of researching topics related to the campus ministry, analyzing the data, and then relating them to the biblical responsibilities of the local church. For instance, chapter four deals with the history of InterVarsity, Navigators, and Campus Crusade. By studying their histories, one can deduce the biblical points that made them successful as well as the weaknesses that led to their compromises and spiritual decline. From such a historic overview, the local church can clearly formulate its mission statement[6] as to what should be included in its campus ministry as well as what it will want to guard against to keep its ministry from becoming a shipwreck of the faith.

DELIMITATIONS

Although this manual is extremely comprehensive, it is not exhaustive. One of its limitations is in chapter two on the historic development of campus ministry. The manual limits the historic overview to primarily English-speaking universities, such as Oxford, Cambridge, St. Andrews, Harvard, Yale, Princeton, and Andover. Further research could be done to include the Lord's work on non-English-speaking campuses. It is tempting to cross over the Neckar River and address the prince, the preacher, and the professor of Heidelberg University or to cross over the Elbe River to address Luther's spiritual development at the University of Wittenberg.[7] Another limitation is in chapter four, where the strengths and

[5]Charles H. Spurgeon, *The Metropolitan Tabernacle Pulpit* (Pasadena, TX: Pilgrim Publications, 1986), 7:364.

[6]The Mission Statement of the Spurgeon Foundation Campus Ministries (SFCM), now Cross Impact Ministries (CIM), adopted on June 23, 1997, states, "The mission of SFCM is to reach college students with the gospel, disciple and train them to fulfill the Great Commission in Matthew 28:19–20 (which includes being baptized), and encourage them to take an active role in the local church by faithful attendance and participation in ministry."

[7]Thea B. Van Halsema, *Three Men Came to Heidelberg* (Grand Rapids: Baker, 1991).

weaknesses of only InterVarsity, Navigators, and Campus Crusade are analyzed. There are more than thirty additional campus ministries that could be similarly studied and critiqued. Another limitation is in chapter six regarding "The Fivefold Scope of Campus Ministry," which includes ministering to undergraduates, graduate students, young married couples, international students, and the faculty and staff of the secular university. This study does not include ministering to the parents and to other family members of the students. Another area omitted is the ministry to the single career person who is no longer in college. This topic has been addressed squarely by Michael D. Cruice in his dissertation, *The Development of a Single Adult Ministry in the Local Fundamental Church.* The chapter on the "Discipleship Goals" of the campus ministry simply presents a practical discipleship plan for the local church and does not give an in-depth treatment of the theology of discipleship.[8] Finally, chapter eleven is a broad overview of the roles of the mission board and the campus ministry. This chapter could be further developed into a manual on the local church and her relationship to the missionary board/sending agency. Strategies and models for campus ministry are described in this manual for the local church and for the statewide/regional aspect of the campus mission board. There are limited details presented to the need of a nationwide mission board that would tie together and unify the statewide/regional aspects of the board, nor is there any development of how to take the campus ministry overseas.

METHOD OF PROCEDURE

There is much written on the history of spiritual awakenings on the campus, student missionary movements, student organizations,

---

[8]The discipleship materials referred to in this section include the author's *The Ploughman's Sower Series, The Ploughman's Harvest Series, The Ploughman's Treasure Series,* and *The Ploughman's Journal and Manual.* Included in these discipleship materials is a topical memory program that includes verses on the Romans Road and verses that coincide with the lessons on discipleship. Also included is a soul-winning plan called "The Gospel Go." Jim Berg's materials (*Basics for Believers, Changed into His Image*), ProTeens (*Ancient Landmarks*), Netcasters, and Dr. Ed Nelson's discipleship materials (*Growing in Grace*) are highly recommended for use with college students.

and the history of colleges and universities.[9] Such historical and biographical works can illustrate key points that are significant to a successful campus ministry based in a local church. However, there is no time in history when all these elements existed, where the local church played the major role in the strategy of campus ministries.

Chapter two presents the evolution of campus ministry, beginning with the ministry of the apostle Paul in Ephesus and ending with the great revivals on the New England campuses of Harvard, Yale, Princeton, Andover, and Williams Colleges. This chapter reveals that in the last five hundred years almost every major awakening, revival, or missions movement can trace its roots to a college campus. This particular section of the manual is a chapter out of church history, with key headings emphasizing the essential elements of a successful campus ministry.

Chapter three departs from the historical backdrop of chapter two and notes the present-day culture of the secular campus. Today the culture on the campus has changed in some ways from the days of the Holy Club at Oxford in the 1700s, but in many ways the campus has not changed. Students are still sinners in need of a Savior. One new irony is that campus ministry is now needed on the campuses of many colleges that once believed and taught the

---

[9]This section of the manual is derived from the biographical studies of some of the heroes of the faith, in which an author records his subject's spiritual incidents while attending college. An example of an outstanding biography is Dallimore's two-volume set on George Whitefield. The first volume has an insightful chapter on Whitefield's conversion experience ("Oxford, the Holy Club and Conversion"; pages 61–77). Issue 52 of *Christian History* magazine has an article entitled "Missions Dream Team" by Alvyn Austin (pages 19–23) that identifies the Cambridge Seven and their exploits after college. George Muller, in his autobiography, describes his conversion experience and growth in grace while attending college. Stuart Piggin's book on *The St. Andrews Seven* is one of the best on that subject. Another work that is helpful in understanding the complex academic settings at Oxford and Cambridge is David Beale's book *The Mayflower Pilgrims* (Greenville, SC: Ambassador-Emerald International, 2000); his listing of the colleges of both universities in the appendices (pages 207 and 209) is especially useful. It is also of interest to note how many of the events in the book *The 100 Most Important Events in Christian History* relate to campus ministry. Such highlights can be compared in Mark Sidwell's *Scenes from American Church History* and in Robert Walton's *Chronological and Background Charts of Church History*. Examples of other biographical studies used in this manual are listed in the bibliography.

Bible. Sadly, such colleges have become the mission field. To reach this secular campus, one must understand the campus culture, including the many "-isms" on campus and the vanity of campus life lived apart from God. The method of study for this chapter involved personal observation; personal interviews of students, faculty, and staff on the secular campus;[10] and much statistical research derived from current periodicals and web sites.[11] The desired result is for the reader to have an accurate view of the present condition of the average secular university and of the desperate need for such campuses to be evangelized. This should lead to a desire to start a campus ministry.

For the church to have an effective ministry on the campus, it must first evaluate and analyze the campus ministry organizational models and decide which one is best suited for its church. Therefore, various organizational models are presented in chapter four, and the advantages and disadvantages of each model are developed. The church's leadership must prayerfully consider which approach matches its burden, vision, and management style. The two most effective models are the missionary model and the college pastor/ missionary model. Once the pastor has counted the cost for the task ahead and has selected the leadership model for the church's outreach, he will need to prepare his church for this ministry. The church's leadership must articulate a clear mission statement defining the goals for the campus ministry (chapter four). These goals are defined by analyzing the strengths and weaknesses of InterVarsity, Navigators, and Campus Crusade. In addition, by studying the rise and fall of these campus ministries, one finds that two ancient landmarks were ignored with each of these groups: accountability to a local church and the doctrine of biblical separation. By emphasizing

---

[10]Personal interviews and surveys were administered to some of the faculty (e.g., Ted Whitwell and Darren Dawson) and their staff at Clemson University to hear firsthand their impressions of the culture of a secular campus (October 2001).

[11]Sources for information on the culture of the college campus include *The Chronicle of Higher Education*, *The Ivy Jungle* (http://www.ivyjungle.org); "Where the Boys Aren't," *U.S. World Report* (February 8, 1999); Bob Jones University's *What in the World*; Bob Jones University's *Balance*; and a variety of newspapers (e.g., http://www.dallasnews.com, http://www.CNSNews.com).

these two doctrines one can avoid the pitfalls of the new evangelical campus organizations. The strength of the fundamental campus ministry is sound doctrine, which must be used to the fundamentalist's advantage and to God's glory.

To have an effective campus ministry, the church must have a campus presence. To have such a presence, the church must charter a student organization. The steps for doing so, as well as other necessary steps in starting a campus ministry, are discussed in chapter five. The chapter also discusses various challenges and hindrances that the local church will face in chartering a campus ministry.

Once the group has been chartered, the doors are opened for the church to fully minister to the fivefold scope of the campus ministry. Chapter six discusses how to identify and meet the needs of each of these five groups.

With over 600,000 international students in America, the majority of whom are from China,[12] India, or other nations with restricted access for Christians (e.g., Muslim nations), ministering to international students is a unique and important part of the campus ministry. God in His wonderful grace has countered Satan's move by bringing these nations' best to America to study. The future leaders of the world are in America's back yard on the college campuses. One of the most effective and efficient ways of reaching the world is to reach international students while they are studying in America. Therefore, chapter seven presents an array of methods for ministering to international students and reaching them with the gospel. In addition, the chapter gives organizational steps for establishing a foreign-speaking church. Chapter eight broadens the study of evangelism to include various methods that are effective in reaching all collegians with the gospel. One evangelistic approach is through

---

[12]A very helpful book on the history of China is Latourette's book *A Short History of the Far East*, which is not so short (776 pages). Carl Lawrence gives good insights to Christianity in China in his book *The Church in China*. One of the better works for ministering to the Chinese on America's colleges is Peter Morrison's book *Making Friends with Mainland Chinese Students*. For a vision for the Orient, a "must read" is Christian Wei's book, *A Bi-lingual University in Mainland China*. The books *God and the Ancient Chinese* and *God's Promises to the Chinese* are exciting resources to use in evangelizing the Chinese. In these two works, the gospel is presented using the picture words of the Chinese.

sports outreaches. Such an approach is defended by the apostle Paul's use of sports metaphors.[13] From the many word studies, a biblical theology for using sports outreaches is developed.

During the past fifty years, discipleship has been strongly associated with campus ministry, perhaps more than with any other discipline within Christian ministry. Once again, the fundamentalist's strength of sound doctrine should be seen on the campus in his approach to discipleship. Therefore, chapter nine delineates practical discipleship goals, strategies, and tools for the campus ministry. Additional tools for conducting a year-round campus ministry are also discussed, with an emphasis on involving students in the ministries of the local church.[14] The true strength of a campus ministry is measured by the degree to which the students are involved in the ministries of the local church and the degree to which the families of the local church involve the students in their own lives. To accomplish these goals an entire chapter (chapter ten) is dedicated to the activities of the campus ministry and the ways students can be involved in the local church.

The need of the hour is for more churches to be planted in college towns and for those established churches near colleges to catch the vision of reaching collegians for Christ. The burden for reaching a state's colleges and universities must be placed on the churches within the school's own state or region. Therefore, this manual presents a strategy for reaching the major universities in each of the fifty states, with an ultimate goal of having a campus presence at all 3,300 colleges in America (chapter eleven). The key for reaching America's campuses involves using the right model for the local

---

[13]This word study is the product of studying and categorizing the metaphors from Paul's writings using A. T. Robertson's *Word Studies of the Greek New Testament*. To describe the Christian life, Paul used military metaphors the most frequently, followed by agricultural metaphors. The third most frequently used type of metaphors was sports metaphors. Paul used a minimum of thirty-three different words drawn from the sports arena.

[14]Navigators uses the *Topical Memory System* (TMS), which is an excellent memory program, for their discipleship. In the 1950s, Billy Graham would always carry the TMS Bible verses in his pocket (Skinner, 322). Dawson Trotman also developed the discipleship tool "The Wheel" (a series of inductive Bible studies) and the booklet *Born to Reproduce*.

church to minister to the secular campus and then developing the state-based/regional aspect of the mission-board model that can be easily duplicated for each state or region. Such models and strategies are presented in this manual at both the local and state levels. The fruit of the statewide/regional aspect of the mission board that targets the major universities within the state will be a greater prayer and financial base for campus workers. At first, such a worker would be classified as a campus pastor/missionary. The worker's organizational loyalty would be first to his local church and then to the mission board. The long-term goal would be for the church to follow church-planting principles so that the worker's full support would ultimately come from his own local church. At that point, the worker's status would be the church's college pastor, and the missionary title and the official ties to the mission board would be dropped. Because the campus pastor/missionary model has never been emphasized or developed in the history of campus ministry, this manual gives careful attention to the role of the senior pastor in managing this model (chapter twelve). In addition, potential problems with this model are also confronted.

Once the burden and vision for campus ministry are seen, the next need is easily discerned: the need for campus pastors, missionaries, and workers. Therefore, the last chapter is an appeal for more campus pastors/missionaries to be called to the neglected mission field of the secular campus. The chapter discusses the necessary call to this ministry and the training needed to undertake the challenge of ministering to the modern-day Athens in America.

Taking the Cross of Christ to the Campus: A Manual for Church-Based Campus Ministry is a comprehensive overview of the spiritual history of student movements, the rise and fall of campus ministries, and the need of the local church to assume the biblical responsibility of fulfilling the Great Commission on America's secular campuses.

2

THE HISTORICAL DEVELOPMENT OF THE CAMPUS MINISTRY

NEW TESTAMENT DAYS— SCHOOL OF TYRANNUS

The Priority of the Church of God

Acts 19:8–10 states,

> And he went into the synagogue, and spake boldly for the space
> of three months, disputing and persuading the things concern-
> ing the kingdom of God. But when divers were hardened, and
> believed not, but spake evil of that way before the multitude, he
> departed from them, and separated the disciples, disputing daily
> in the school of one Tyrannus. And this continued by the space
> of two years; so that all they which dwelt in Asia heard the word
> of the Lord Jesus, both Jews and Greeks.

The roots for campus ministry are found in Acts 19:8–10, with the
apostle Paul ministering at Tyrannus University (TU). One of Paul's
most effective church-planting projects took place at Ephesus at TU
and provides a noteworthy pattern. Paul sought first to convince
his Jewish friends that the carpenter's son from Nazareth was indeed the promised Messiah but was asked to move his schoolroom
elsewhere. They had heard enough of this Jesus who Paul declared
had died for their sins and was raised from the dead on the third
day. Consequently, Paul sought for a strategic place to reach people
with the gospel and to plant a church. The ideal place was to take
up shop at "the school of one Tyrannus"[1] (Acts 19:9). Tyrannus was

---

[1] John McRay, *Archaeology and the New Testament* (Grand Rapids: Baker, 1991),
261. McRay states, "One of the most prominent civic structures in Ephesus was

either the owner of the school or its most famous Dean of Doom, "the Tyrant." It is interesting to note that Codex Bezae reads that "Paul argued daily in the hall of Tyrannus from the fifth hour to the tenth."[2] If this is accurate, having been preserved in oral tradition and then incorporated in the text of certain manuscripts, Paul taught daily from 11:00 a.m. to 4:00 p.m. Regardless, the result of Paul's ministry, which had its epicenter in Ephesus at an institution of higher learning, was that "all they which dwelt in Asia [Minor] heard the word of the Lord Jesus."[3]

It is possible that the seven churches of the book of Revelation were also founded at this time. How could the gospel spread so quickly and pervasively into the world? How much did Paul's choosing to meet at the "hall of Tyrannus" factor into such rapid growth of the church? Are there any parallels in church history that indicate that America's "learning halls" are the ripest seedbeds for evangelism, revival, and recruiting volunteers for world evangelism? Church history suggests that one of the most strategic sites to target ministry is on the college campus, secular or religious. In fact, the church can trace much of her growth in the past four hundred years to various student movements. It is important to note that whatever ministry Paul had to the students at the "hall of Tyrannus," it was based out of a local church context. One of the greatest errors in campus ministry throughout the church age is to divorce the campus ministry from the institution of the local church.

---

the Library of Celsus, the subject of a recent and impressive reconstruction at its site south of the lower agora. Built to honor Gaius Julius Celsus Polemaeanus by his son, according to Greek and Latin inscriptions on the wings of the front steps, the library was begun in AD 110 and finished in 135. Celsus was consul in 92 and later proconsul of Asia. Ekrem Akurgal locates an auditorium or lecture hall just east of the front of the library. The hall is mentioned in a first-century inscription and is noteworthy because Luke states that Paul reasoned daily in Ephesus in the hall or school of Tyrannus. Colin J. Hemer has argued that the Greek words for *auditorium* and *school* were virtually synonymous. The 'Auditorium' is a subject of discussion, but little, if any, of the actual structure has been uncovered, although portions of a circular Hellenistic platform destroyed when the auditorium was constructed have been revealed."

[2]F. F. Bruce, *The New International Commentary on the New Testament: The Book of the Acts* (Grand Rapids: Eerdmans, 1988), 365.

[3]Acts 19:10.

STUDENT MOVEMENTS IN ENGLISH-SPEAKING EUROPE

The Primacy of the Word of God

In the fourteenth century (1320–1384), at Oxford University, the oldest English-speaking college in the world, there was a man by the name of John Wycliffe, who influenced all English-speaking Christians with his English translation of the Bible. Later the King James Version was produced by the translators at Westminster Abbey (where they translated Genesis through 2 Kings), Cambridge University (where they translated 1 Chronicles through Song of Solomon and the Apocrypha), and Oxford University (where they translated Isaiah through Acts and the book of Revelation). A second committee at Westminster Abbey translated and revised Romans through Jude.

As early as 1523 Thomas Bilney and his friends met secretly at the White Horse Inn at Cambridge University. Such student meetings had at their heart the study of Scriptures, the foundational textbook for any campus ministry. One can imagine Hugh Latimer reading his Greek New Testament in the candlelight and articulating the doctrine of justification as he read from the works of Martin Luther. Why was there the need for Christian students to meet secretly on the campuses of universities that were linked with the church? Why, in April of 1554 at the University Church of St. Mary, did the Divinity School at Oxford charge Latimer and Nicholas Ridley with heresy? What was heretical about Latimer's defense that "Christ made one perfect sacrifice for all the world. . . . Neither is there propitiation for our sins, saving his cross only"?[4] Why on October 16, 1555, would a godly Hugh Latimer and a faithful Nicholas Ridley be burned at the stake at Oxford University followed by three hundred others? The answer: education, divorced from the Word of God, sharpens the attack on the people of God. Ironically, Oxford's original coat of arms contained an "ox" crossing a "ford" with *Fortis est Veritas* (Mighty is Truth) on the bottom. Oxford, the oldest English-speaking university in the world, was no longer mighty in

---

[4]David Beale, *The Mayflower Pilgrims* (Greenville, SC: Ambassador-Emerald International, 2000), 194.

truth. The ox had sadly crossed over the "ford" and has been looking for the shoreline of "mystery Babylon"[5] ever since.

Not all those who taught at Oxford or at Cambridge, Great Britain's second oldest university, had yielded to deism or unbelief. There were those over the years who were "of good courage" and "played the man."[6] There was Thomas Cartwright, professor of divinity, who took his stand and was forced into exile in Geneva. Cartwright would contend for the faith and even challenged the *Book of Common Prayer*, calling it "an imperfect book, culled and picked out of the popish dunghill."[7] Influenced at Cambridge by the Presbyterian Puritan Thomas Cartwright was Robert Browne. This student would be the first on England's shores to call for separation of church and state. Later in 1588, Francis Johnson followed in the footsteps of Cartwright and was imprisoned for his application of the text of 1 Peter 5:1–4. Another Cambridge separatist of that era was John Penry, who was known as the Morning Star of the Reformation in Wales. Penry would be placed in the "Clink" Prison and hanged for his separatist convictions. Dr. John Reynolds, president of Corpus Christi College at Oxford, argued for his Puritan convictions. Richard Clyfton, a graduate of Christ's College, Cambridge, influenced William Bradford with his separatist beliefs. Another graduate of Christ's College was John Smyth, who ministered in London. While studying at Cambridge, William Brewster was influenced by John Penry, Francis Johnson, John Greenwood, and the converted drunk William Perkins. Men such as these laid the groundwork for the Mayflower pilgrimage and the separatist movement in England and America. Roger Williams, the founder of the first Baptist church in America, was a graduate of Pembroke College, Cambridge, receiving his B.A. degree in 1627. Williams contended that the Church of England was apostate, that King Charles I resembled more the Beast in the book of Revelation than a Christian, that the colonies should cease forcing unsaved people to attend church, that there should be a separation between

---

[5]Rev. 17:5.
[6]Beale, *The Mayflower Pilgrims*, 194.
[7]Ibid., 9.

church and state, and that the Indians were the rightful owners of the land. Puritan theologians William Ames and Thomas Goodwin studied at Christ's College. As can be seen, Cambridge University played a prominent role in the Protestant Reformation with such students as Desiderius Erasmus, William Tyndale, Hugh Latimer, and Thomas Cranmer. Puritans, Presbyterians, Congregationalists, and even Baptists can trace their roots to Cambridge University, the nursery of English Puritanism. Sadly, schools like Oxford and Cambridge have fulfilled the earlier prophecy of Martin Luther, who said, "Every institution where men are not unceasingly occupied with the Word of God must become corrupt."[8]

The Holy Club at Oxford—1700s
The Preeminence of the Righteousness of God

"A brand plucked out of the fire"[9] was John Wesley, who, following his father's and grandfathers' footsteps, tramped off to Oxford University in 1721 at the age of 17, matriculating from Christ Church College. At Oxford, John, religious but lost, pursued the ministry and was ordained as a deacon in Christ Church Cathedral and later as a priest (minister). While John was serving a curacy at Wroot, his younger brother Charles, a King's scholar, entered Oxford in 1726 at the age of 19. Charles's first year at Oxford was a difficult year for him, as it is for many college students. He did not seek "the pleasures of sin"[10] at Oxford, which were many, but he also did not seek the Lord. Later he would describe Oxford University in these words:

> Where learning keeps its loftiest seat,
> And hell its firmest throne.[11]

On another occasion he wrote,

> Bolder I with my fellows grew,
> Nor yet to evil ran,

---

[8]Paul Lee Tan, *Encyclopedia of 7,700 Illustrations: Signs of the Times* (Rockville, MD: Assurance Publishers, 1979), 159.

[9]Zech. 3:2.

[10]Heb. 11:25.

[11]Arnold Dallimore, *George Whitefield* (Carlisle, PA: Banner of Truth, 1979), 1:64.

But envied those who dared break through,
And copy lawless man;
From parents' eye far off removed,
I still was under Thine,
And found, for secret sin reproved,
The government divine.[12]

Thomas Sheridan stated that Oxford taught "a continuation of the classics learned at school, the rudiments of logic, natural philosophy, astronomy, metaphysics and heathen morality thrown in."[13] According to Charles Wesley, "my first year at college I lost in diversions."[14] Admittedly, his biggest diversion was the young ladies who lived in the villages of Buckland, Broadway, and Stanton.

The following school year, Charles gave up the girls and dedicated himself to "serious thinking" and to pursuing a disciplined, religious life as an ordained deacon, which earned him the name "the Methodist." Charles was able to influence several of his friends to accompany him in such a disciplined lifestyle, resulting in the inauguration of the Holy Club in 1728 with three members: Robert Kirkham, William Morgan, and Charles Wesley. This was not the first such campus club, for there were other student religious societies elsewhere, such as the Collegia Pietatis of Germany.

When John returned to tutor at Lincoln College, he was asked to be the Holy Club's head. The Holy Club members specialized in maximizing every second of their lives to do good, with the end result being to merit God's favor. At nightfall each member examined how he spent his day and then wrote his failures and wasted seconds in his journal. He was then to write out his plan on how he was going to be more devout the next day. The Holy Club members studied their Greek New Testaments daily; fasted on Wednesdays and Fridays; attended the sacrament every Sunday; weekly ministered at two prisons, the Bocardo and the Castle; and sacrificially gave their alms to the underprivileged. John would seldom sleep

---

[12]Arnold Dallimore, *A Heart Set Free* (London: Evangelical Press, 1991), 33.

[13]Dallimore, *George Whitefield*, 63.

[14]Dallimore, *A Heart Set Free*, 33.

past 4:00 a.m. and would write his mother to tell her that he was "full of business" and noted that "idleness slays."[15]

Adding to the unusual mix at Oxford was George Whitefield, who, on November 7, 1732, matriculated at Pembroke College as a servitor. A servitor received free tuition in exchange for doing much of the dirty work for the highly placed students. Whitefield was a serious student who had no time for fellow students who were indolent. He wrote in his journal, "It has often grieved my soul to see so many young students spending their substance in extravagant living, and thereby entirely unfitting themselves for the prosecution of their studies."[16] Whitefield could not be tempted to join the partying of his roommates and consequently found himself extremely lonely until he came in contact with one of the despised Methodists whom his roommates had mocked, calling them Bible Moths, Bible Bigots, and other names. Violating the guidelines of a servitor, Whitefield met with this upperclassman, who would later write of their first encounter in these poetic words:

> Can I the memorable day forget,
> When first we by Divine appointment met?
> Where undisturbed the thoughtful student roves
> In search of truth, through academic groves;
> A modest, pensive youth, who mused alone,
> Industrious the frequented path to shun,
> An Israelite without disguise or art,
> I saw, I loved, and clasped him to my heart,
> A stranger as my bosom-friend caress'd,
> And unawares received an angel-guest.[17]

This breakfast engagement with Charles Wesley was the beginning of a new chapter for George Whitefield. At first George was a little embarrassed being seen with Charles but quickly entered into the Holy Club's services.

---

[15]Skevington Wood, *The Burning Heart* (Minneapolis, MN: Bethany Fellowship, 1967), 41–42.

[16]Dallimore, *George Whitefield*, 64.

[17]Ibid., 66.

It was there at Oxford that John and Charles followed their father's and grandfathers' footsteps and studied to be ministers. It was there at Oxford that they sought to perform devotedly to find acceptance with God. It was there at Oxford that they still came up empty. It was there at Oxford that they yielded to what they perceived as the ultimate acceptance path and the greatest act of self-denial: to be missionaries to savages in the newest of England's colonies, Georgia. Their ministry in Georgia was more stormy than the trip to and fro. Charles returned to England first and was verbally spanked by his mother for such a foolish adventure, she forbade him to go to Georgia again.

While in London, Charles conversed with a man who talked about the necessity of the new birth, an inward change. Kezia, his sister, said that "she believed now there was such a thing as a new creature . . . that she was not, but longed to be converted."[18] The arrow that pierced his empty heart was his visits to hear his former Holy Club friend George Whitefield, who had been converted at Oxford in 1735, preach to the throngs on the need of being born again. Also convicting were the frequent challenges of the Moravian Peter Bohler, who was carving away at the Wesleys' doctrine of salvation by works. At one point, he told John Wesley to "Preach faith till you have it, and then, because you have it, you will preach faith."[19] Charles discovered that Bohler's message of justification by faith was the chief teaching of Martin Luther. This confirmed the doctrine for Charles. On May 21, 1738, Pentecost Sunday in the Church of England, Charles Wesley was born again, resisting no longer the Spirit of Pentecost. Charles penned his conversion hymn on May 23, 1738, and a year later he penned these words on the first anniversary of his conversion:

> And can it be that I should gain
> An interest in the Saviour's blood?
> Died he for me, who caused his pain?
> For me who Him to death pursued?
> Amazing love! How can it be
> That thou, my God, shouldst die for me?[20]

---

[18]Dallimore, *A Heart Set Free*, 57.
[19]Ibid., 59.
[20]Ibid., 62.

After Charles's conversion, John wrote, "I received the surprising news that my brother had found rest to his soul."[21] The following day John also found rest for his soul as he experienced the heartwarming experience in Aldersgate Street on May 24, 1738. God saved the musician and songwriter before the messenger.

As Arnold Dallimore summarizes, the Holy Club was not famous at first and was hardly known on campus.[22] It was not evangelical in nature. They did not preach the gospel but taught a works salvation and adopted a view of the Lord's Supper bordering the heresy of transubstantiation. Consequently, the Holy Club did not produce revival but death; and with the dispersal of its members in 1735, the club also died. It also did not bring the joy and peace that its members longed for. In reality, it brought even greater dissatisfaction. In many ways the Holy Club at Oxford was the schoolmaster that brought the Wesleys and Whitefield to Christ. Often Whitefield would refer to Oxford on his spiritual birth certificate. In a sermon entitled "All Men's Place" he declared, "I know the place! It may be superstitious, perhaps, but whenever I go to Oxford I cannot help running to that place where Jesus Christ first revealed himself to me and gave me the new birth."[23] Today, there are still some on the college campus who have enrolled in the Holy Club of self-righteousness and who need to transfer their faith to Christ and mark the spot of their new birth. Two continents were awakened by the ministry of the men of the Holy Club. How many Whitefields are enrolled in America's colleges today seeking for "The Life of God in the Soul of Man"?[24]

The St. Andrews Seven
The Participation with the Spirit of God

Scotland's oldest university is St. Andrews. While Oxford emphasized the classics and Cambridge emphasized mathematics, St. Andrews's forte was philosophy. Such an academic setting was conducive for the life work of the St. Andrews Seven, comprised of its

---

[21]Ibid.

[22]*George Whitefield*, 71–72.

[23]Ibid., 77.

[24]*The Life of God in the Soul of Man*, by Henry Scougal, was a book instrumental in challenging Whitefield to be saved.

famous six students and their faculty advisor. The St. Andrews Seven were Professor Thomas Chalmers, Alexander Duff, John Urquhart, John Adam, Robert Nesbit, William Sinclair Mackay, and David Ewart. All were accomplished scholars, winning many scholarships and academic prizes. They were, from an academic viewpoint, extremely credible witnesses to the grace of God. But more importantly, the St. Andrews Seven prayed, studied the Scriptures, and challenged their peers to trust Christ. The result of such labors was St. Andrews's largest student society being formed in the 1820s. They were so successful that the enemies of truth started a counter-organization.

When Thomas Chalmers came to St. Andrews in 1823 to teach the two hundred enrolled students, he had a clear-cut testimony of salvation. In a letter dated February 14, 1820, to his brother Alexander, he wrote,

> I am now most thoroughly of opinion, and it is an opinion founded on experience, that on the system of Do this and live, no peace, and even no true and worthy obedience, can ever be attained. It is, Believe in the Lord Jesus Christ, and thou shalt be saved. When this belief enters the heart, joy and confidence enter along with it. The righteousness which we try to work out for ourselves eludes our impotent grasp, and never can a soul arrive at true or permanent rest in the pursuit of this object. The righteousness which, by faith, we put on, secures our acceptance with God, and secures our interest in His promises and gives us a part in those sanctifying influences by which we are enabled to do with aid from on high what we never can do without it. We become new creatures in Jesus Christ our Lord.[25]

However, the spiritual condition at St. Andrews was dark at this time. The scriptures were mocked, and the chapel was dead. Forty-three-year-old Chalmers brought life, enthusiasm, and conviction to the classroom. The previously mentioned six students progressed in particular. John Urquhart, the youngest of the St. Andrews Seven, was born again under the ministry of Congregationalist William

---

[25]Stuart Piggin and John Roxborogh, *The St. Andrews Seven* (Carlisle, PA: Banner of Truth, 1985), 4–5.

Orme just before coming to St. Andrews. Urquhart wrote to his pastor:

> My first impression of danger, as a sinner, was caused by a ser-
> mon you preached on a Lord's day evening. . . . At that time, I
> was very much affected; it was then, I think, that I first really
> prayed. I retired to my apartment, and with many tears con-
> fessed my guilt before God.[26]

The most conspicuous of the St. Andrews Seven was Alexander Duff, who also was saved before coming to college but needed someone to mentor him spiritually. Then there was Robert Nesbit, the oldest of the group, who by diligence rather than brilliance found himself at the top of his class. Prior to attending St. Andrews, he was unsaved and appallingly self-righteous. It took the drowning of his brother at sea for him to ask himself if he were the one to have drowned, would he have gone to heaven. Having no assurance that he would and convicted that he had no power over his sins, he realized that he needed the grace of God and His righteousness. John Adam came to St. Andrews with a rich evangelical background, while David Ewart and William Sinclair Mackay brought a strong physique and intellectual gifts to the mix. Thomas Chalmers had much to work with in these students.

Chalmers took a great interest in his students and these six in particular, having them over for dinner frequently. The Doctor would
challenge the students to excel in their studies. He instructed his
students that

> It is by dint of steady labor - it is by giving enough of application
> to the work, and having enough of time for the doing of it - it
> is by regular painstaking and the constant assiduities - it is by
> these, and not by any process of legerdemain, that we secure the
> strength and the staple of real excellence.[27]

This advice they took to heart, resulting in their capturing most of the academic awards at the end of the school year. If one searches the Library receipt books, one would note that Alexander Duff

---

[26]Ibid., 15.
[27]Ibid., 32.

alone checked out 334 titles and 413 volumes from the library.[28] The St. Andrews Seven did not ignore the "wisdom of the Egyptians";[29] however, each prided himself in being a *homo unius libri*, the Bible.

The St. Andrews Seven had intellect on fire. They had received a solid academic base in research, analysis, and synthesis and had made the Bible the touchstone of all truth. The vehicle for applying their Biblical knowledge was the formation of the St. Andrews Missionary Society on December 6, 1824. These students knew that it was their responsibility to preach the gospel and that it was God the Holy Spirit's responsibility to do the regenerating. The question for them now was where to direct this gospel machine. They heeded the suggestion to study the missionary model of the Baptist missionary William Carey. Despite the lack of support from most of the faculty and administration at St. Andrews and the difficulty of finding a room large enough for the 70 of the school's 320 students to meet in, the student organization moved forward.

Once again Thomas Chalmers came to the rescue and stood with the students despite the opposition towards their organization and their desire to go into all the world to preach the gospel. Wisely, Chalmers invited dynamic and successful missionaries, such as Joshua Marshman of the Baptist Missionary Society and Robert Morrison and Henry Townley of the London Missionary Society, to come speak to the students. The St. Andrews Seven were benefiting by such "block" classes on missions taught by experienced missionaries. In addition, the society purchased missionary biographies and assigned members to give reports on them. In 1831, Alexander Duff recorded the impact of such a discipline: "Well can I trace the dawn, the rise, and progress of any feeble missionary spirit I possess, to the readings, conversations, and essays called for by the student Missionary Association in St. Andrews."[30] The missionary association met on the first Monday of each month at 5:00 p.m. and was very well organized. Students such as Henry Craik attended such meetings. Craik would later join George Muller in Germany

---

[28]Ibid., 35.

[29]Acts 7:22.

[30]Piggin and Roxborogh, *The St. Andrews Seven*, 48.

to serve the Lord at the orphanage. John Adam wrote on November 22, 1825,

> From seven to nine in the evening I am engaged with J. Urquhart in collecting, under specific heads, all possible information on the subject of missions, both from Scriptures, under the titles of precepts - prophecies - promises - and examples, and from all other books whatever we can lay our hands on; the object of this is, with our united prayers, to seek a sober determination of the inquiry, whether or not we ought to embark in this enterprise.[31]

After studying Carey's approach to missions and gathering as much biblical information as possible, the society sought where they should seek to minister with some of its members. Urquhart, the president of the society, preached to eighty of the students and challenged them to find God's will and do it. Shortly afterwards, he became ill and died on January 10, 1827. This event stirred the hearts of all those in the society and caused them to take Urquhart's challenge to surrender to missions even more to heart. Six months after Urquhart's death, Robert Nesbit departed for India. The second of the St. Andrews Seven to sail to India was John Adam, then Duff, followed by William Sinclair Mackay and finally by the last of the St. Andrews Seven, David Ewart. By 1857, over five hundred British missionaries had gone to serve in India. One tenth of such missionaries were Scottish Presbyterians who could trace their roots back to the St. Andrews Seven. "Together the St. Andrews 'Six' gave 141 years service to the missionary cause. Urquhart had made a wise investment of his eighteen years."[32] Alexander Duff became the most renowned missionary in India's history after William Carey. Duff started a college in Calcutta, which became the model for missionaries to follow. It was Duff who targeted teaching the Indians of the higher caste a full curriculum in English centered in the truths of the Bible. Who was Duff's model for such a school? It was none other than Thomas Chalmers of St. Andrews!

---

[31] Ibid., 70.
[32] Ibid., 111.

The Cambridge Seven—1800s
The Promotion of the Work of God

From the 1400s to the 1700s the college campuses in Great Britain played a large role in English Bible translations, printing of Bibles (with the printing divisions of Oxford and Cambridge leading the way), the great awakenings, Puritanism, separatism, and other areas. In the 1800s, a new role for campus ministries developed in Great Britain: colleges were not only a target for evangelism but also a very fertile ground for recruiting missionary volunteers. However, this change does not imply that the college campus had not yet produced a successful missionary. Predating both William Carey, "the Father of Modern Missions," and Adoniram Judson was the "Apostle to the Indians," John Eliot. Eliot studied for the ministry at Cambridge University from 1618 to 1622; however, he was not saved because of the teaching at Cambridge but as a result of his time spent with a Puritan clergyman, Thomas Hooker. Eliot wrote, "Here the Lord said to my dead soul, Live! Live! And through the grace of God I do live and shall live forever! When I came to this blessed family I then saw as never before, the power of godliness in its lovely vigor and efficacy."[33] Hooker was forced to flee to Holland for his Puritan convictions. Seeing the handwriting on the wall, Eliot and his fiancée fled to America. John pastored in Boston, but his heart was burdened for the Algonquin Indians. Due to the strong linguistic training John received at Cambridge, he was able to learn the Algonquin language quickly, despite the fact that there was no written grammar or dictionary. Once he learned the tongue of the Algonquins, he began to preach the gospel to the natives, and soon there was fruit. Eliot's converts were called "praying Indians." With the "praying Indians," Eliot established "praying villages" and soon trained "praying Indian preachers" in his "praying schools," but perhaps his greatest contribution was the translation of the entire Bible into Algonquin in 1663. Eliot's Algonquin Bible was the first Bible to roll off an American press. Truly when John Eliot went to be with the Lord on May 20, 1690, he left behind the model and

---

[33]Mark Sidwell, *Faith of our Fathers: Scenes from American Church History* (Greenville, SC: Bob Jones University Press, 1991), 18.

the goals for all future mission work to follow. It was this model that seven men from Cambridge would seek to imitate in the 1800s.

D. L. Moody had tremendous spiritual freedom to preach to the college students at Cambridge University. As a result of the revival at Cambridge, one of the students converted during an evangelistic service with Moody founded a student organization called the Cambridge Christian Union. This student, Stanley Peregrine Smith, was a man's man, the captain of the Cambridge rowing team and a man of high energy. Alongside of Stanley Smith stood a revived C. T. Studd, the captain of the cricket team. During the Moody revival, he had gotten things right with the Lord and had the joy of his salvation restored to him. Studd said,

> Instead of going and telling others of the love of Christ, I was selfish and kept the knowledge to myself. The result was that gradually my love began to grow cold, and the love of the world began to come in. I spent six years in that unhappy backslidden state.[34]

Smith was called the "percussion cap" and the revived C. T. Studd the "Roman candle." C. T. stated that the "Lord set me to work for Him, and I began to try and persuade my friends to read the Gospel, and to speak to them individually about their souls."[35] Studd was successful in his persuasion, and after winning his first convert, he wrote,

> I cannot tell you what joy it gave me to bring the first soul to the Lord Jesus Christ. I have tasted almost all the pleasures that this world can give. I do not suppose there is one that I have not experienced, but I can tell you that those pleasures were as nothing to the joy that the saving of that one soul gave me.[36]

Another member of the Cambridge Seven was "Will the Silent" Wharton Cassels, an ordained Anglican minister who was a "Holy Club" man but with the indwelling Spirit to match. Dixon Hoste was another member on the Mission Dream Team who loved order

---

[34]Norman Grubb, *C. T. Studd: Cricketer and Pioneer* (Fort Washington, PA: Christian Literature Crusade, 1982), 31.

[35]Ibid., 33.

[36]Ibid.

and precision. He too had been converted during the Moody revival. Then there were two brothers: Cecil and Arthur Polhill-Turner, a lieutenant in the Royal Dragoons and a priest respectively. Completing the team was Montague Beauchamp, who was as rich and colorful as his name. These seven men, known as the Cambridge Seven, volunteered to go to China and departed for Shanghai in February 1885. In Shanghai they met Hudson Taylor, who divided the team and delegated responsibilities to each.

While in China, C. T. Studd received word that he had inherited a fortune worth several million dollars by today's standards. His response was to give it all away. He gave one fifth to Mr. Moody, which was later used to start the Moody Bible Institute in Chicago; one fifth to Mr. George Muller and his orphanage; one fifth to George Holland in Whitechapel to assist in his ministry among the poor of London; and one fifth to the Salvation Army in India. Then he sent the last fifth to five other servants of the Lord. After serving as a missionary in China and then in India, C. T. Studd traveled to America to visit the American universities with the purpose of further encouraging the Student Volunteer Movement, which was a student organization composed of college students burdened for world evangelism. Then in 1910 he initiated the missionary push to evangelize the region between the Nile and Lake Chad, which was the largest unevangelized region in Africa at that time. At the age of fifty, he founded the Heart of Africa Mission and served the Lord until his death in 1931 in the Belgian Congo. Cecil Polhill-Turner followed Studd's lead of pioneering new mission fields and founded the Tibetan Border Mission.

As a result of the Cambridge Seven's willingness to go to China, the China Inland Mission (CIM) was catapulted from obscurity to "almost embarrassing prominence."[37] The example of these visionaries led hundreds of other students and volunteers to give their lives to world evangelism. In 1885, when the Cambridge Seven arrived in China, the CIM had 163 missionaries; by 1890 the number of CIM missionaries reached 800, and by 1900 one third of the entire Protestant missionary force was represented by the CIM. The

---

[37]Alvyn Austin, "Missions Dream Team," *Christian History*, November 1996, 19.

Cambridge Seven not only impacted missions to China but also directly opened new doors to India and Africa. Today, do fundamentalists need volunteers for world evangelism? Are fundamentalists working the fields of the college campuses for future recruits?

STUDENT RELIGIOUS MEETINGS AND SOCIETIES IN AMERICA

The Prayer for the Servants of God
Harvard University

In America, eighty-eight of the first one hundred colleges were organized to preach the gospel.[38] In 1636 Harvard College, the first of these colleges, was founded in Cambridge, Massachusetts, by Puritans who had the goal of training ministers of the gospel. The mission statement for the college was stated by John Harvard, who gave a large sum of money to start the college: "Let every student be plainly instructed and earnestly pressed to consider well the main ends of this life and studies; to know God and Jesus Christ, which is eternal life."[39] In the Harvard student handbook adopted in 1646, one rule read: "Every one shall exercise himself in reading the Scriptures twice a day that they be ready to give an account of their proficiency therein, both in theoretical observations and logic, and in practical and spiritual truths."[40] In the 1600s, fifty-two percent of Harvard's graduates entered into the full-time ministry of the Word. Sadly, like Oxford, Harvard began to let its "Orthodox Ox" cross back over "the ford." In the years that followed, the university drifted from the vision of its founders and became intolerant to those who held to its puritanical roots. Consequently, students met in secret to exercise their spiritual muscles. The first record of an organized student religious meeting in America was dated January 10, 1723. It was called "The Private Meeting Instituted at Harvard College" and was attended by twenty-six students. As a result of secret student meetings, such as the Private Meeting and the Aldelph Theologia at Harvard, the Religious Society at Dartmouth College,

---

[38]Tan, *Illustrations*, 157.
[39]Ibid., 158.
[40]Ibid.

The College Praying Society at Brown College, the Rising Sun and the Brethren Society at Williams College, the Society for Inquiry Concerning Missions at Andover Theological College, the Society for Religious Revivals at Vermont College and the Philadelphia Society of Princeton University, sixteen additional colleges with spiritual emphases were founded in the 1700s. This fact highlights another by-product of campus ministry: the pioneering and founding of educational institutions.

Revivals at Yale University and Princeton University

In 1701, Yale College was founded in New Haven, Connecticut, by Congregationalists. Fifteen years later, twelve-year-old Jonathan Edwards matriculated at Yale. The young Edwards was saved to enjoy "sweet delight in God and divine things" just after his graduation at Yale and prior to his return to Yale in 1722 to pursue his master's degree.[41] Edwards would be known as the man who fueled the Great Awakening with his sermon "Sinners in the Hands of an Angry God" preached in 1741. In 1757, Edwards became the president of the College of New Jersey, known as Princeton University.

After Yale graduate Jonathan Edwards, the next leading American preacher of the Great Awakening was Gilbert Tennent. Gilbert's father William, educated at Edinburgh University, pioneered for his children the little Log College, which was a twenty-foot by twenty-foot building of logs in Neshaminy, Pennsylvania. All thirteen members of the Log College's first class became the pioneers of Christian education in America. The founders of some fifty-one colleges were graduates of the Log College.[42] After the death of William Tennent Sr., the school was moved to New Jersey and was called the College of New Jersey, now known as Princeton University. Gilbert Tennent did his master's work at Yale and graduated in 1725. Gilbert's most famous sermon, based on Mark 6:34, was entitled "The Danger of the Unconverted Ministry." Gilbert's great fear was that there were too many pastors ministering who were unconverted themselves and who needed to come to the realization, as did John Wesley, that

---

[41]Sidwell, *Faith of Our Fathers*, 34.
[42]Ibid., 41.

they needed to be converted. It was said of Gilbert Tennent by Dr. Samuel Finley that "above other things, the purity of the ministry was his care; and . . . he zealously urged every scriptural method, by which carnal and earthly-minded men might be kept from entering into it."[43] Oxford graduate and the major human instrument in America's Great Awakening, George Whitefield, said of Gilbert's message, "Hypocrites must either soon be converted or enraged."[44]

Revivals would continue at Yale depending on its leadership. The leading revivals were under the leadership of Timothy Dwight, who challenged the students to be saved and surrendered to the will of God. In 1814 he advised the student body, "Christ is the only, the true, the living way of access to God. Give up yourselves to him, with a cordial confidence, and the great work of life is done."[45] Revivals at Yale influenced men to indeed "Give themselves up to Christ." Two of the men influenced by these revivals were Borden of Yale and Asahel Nettleton, who surrendered to the Lord during the revival at Yale in 1807 to 1808.

Similar messages of consecration and surrender to Christ were preached at Princeton by its earlier godly presidents. John Witherspoon, president of Princeton, stated his philosophy of education in these words: "Cursed be all learning that is contrary to the cross of Christ. Cursed be all learning that is not coincident with the cross of Christ. Cursed be all learning that is not subservient to the cross of Christ."[46] One of the non-graduating students at Princeton in the 1780s was a "full-blooded negro of dark brown complexion," John Chavis.[47] Chavis attended Princeton to be trained for the pulpit ministry of the Presbyterian movement. Some say Chavis attended Princeton to settle a bet that a black person could not learn Latin and Greek. If such a story is true, someone lost the bet! Chavis returned from Princeton to minister in Virginia and North Carolina as a highly equipped servant of the Lord. His

---

[43]Tan, *Illustrations*, 42.

[44]Sidwell, *Faith of Our Fathers*, 42.

[45]Tan, *Illustrations*, 158.

[46]Ibid.

[47]Sidwell, *Faith of Our Fathers*, 79.

philosophy for educating his black friends was summarized in these words: "Those who think proper to put their children under my care may rely upon the strictest attention being paid not only to their education but to their morals which I determine an important part of their education."[48]

The Haystack Revival at Williams College
In 1806, five students at Williams College in Massachusetts were overtaken in a thunderstorm during their prayer meeting and sought shelter under a nearby haystack. While waiting out the storm, the five talked about the need of world evangelism and how someone needed to go into the world and preach the gospel. Suddenly, Samuel Mills came up with the "novel" idea of "Why should we not be the ones?" Luther Rice and the other three students agreed that this was a great idea. Rice would later be one of the key leaders for the Baptists in foreign missions, and Samuel Mills would eventually lead the Congregationalists to form the American Board of Commissioners for Foreign Missions, America's first foreign mission board. Such campus groups as those at Williams College were formed to promote devotional life, theological thinking, evangelism, and missions. These student groups helped spawn organizations such as the YMCA and the Student Volunteer Movement (SVM). Just the SVM, conceived in 1886 at a conference led by D. L. Moody in Mount Hermon, Massachusetts, sent out approximately 4,500 missionaries between 1899 and 1914; in addition, within its history, the SVM has motivated approximately 20,000 North American students to become missionaries.

Adoniram Judson of Andover Theological College
The first answer to the prayer of the Williams College students who waited out the storm in a haystack and prayed for volunteers for foreign missions was Adoniram Judson, the son of a Yale graduate. At age sixteen Adoniram chose to attend Rhode Island College at Providence (later called Brown University) because Yale was too far away and Harvard had become too liberal. Once Adoniram arrived in Providence, he had very little interest in spiritual things and was

---

[48]Ibid., 81.

influenced by many to doubt his rich spiritual heritage and the orthodox preaching of his father. The man who influenced him the most was Jacob Eames, a witty and brilliant student who had little time for God. If pressed, he would theologically align himself with Voltaire, Paine, Franklin, and other deists. Soon, Adoniram was corrupted by his peer and became a deist. Eames graduated a year before Judson, but the damage was done, as is so often the case for students during their college days.

Judson graduated top in his class and gave the valedictorian speech, the last of eighteen speeches. After graduation, Adoniram wanted to see the world and to experience the "pleasures of sin for a season."[49] After spending "his substance" and the substance of others, Judson finally "came to himself"[50] when he was confronted with the piety and grace of a young minister about his age. Under conviction, he turned from the attractions of New York City and headed home to Plymouth. On the way home he stayed one night in an inn. The innkeeper told him that the only room he had was next to a room where a man was dying. Judson was not picky, but that night he slept restlessly as he heard the person on the other side of the wall groaning, obviously in deep pain. Once morning came, Judson checked out of the inn and asked curiously if the sick man was feeling any better. The innkeeper said that the man had died during the night. Judson asked if the innkeeper knew who the man was. Judson's countenance fell to the floor when he heard that the dead man was a young graduate from Brown University by the name of Jacob Eames. All he could think of was his friend dead and lost for eternity. When Judson returned home, his father introduced him to the two professors at a new school, Andover Theological Seminary that had just been incorporated the year before. These two Yale graduates made arrangements for Judson to attend Andover as a special student since he had no salvation testimony. On October 12, Judson started his career at this college with a two-man faculty. Two months later, on December 12, 1808, Judson "made a solemn

---

[49]Heb. 11:25.
[50]Luke 15:17.

dedication of himself to God."[51] It was on this day that Judson gave his heart to the Lord, either in salvation or assurance of salvation. Regardless, he was now the Lord's, and what mattered most to Judson was to do the Lord's will. God's will for the Andover graduate was to be America's first missionary to a foreign field, the golden shore of Burma. Judson was not the only student at this time who surrendered his heart to God on the college campus to missions, nor would he be the last.

At Andover in 1811, a student organization was formed called the Andover Seminary Society of Enquiry, which was designed to challenge every divinity student with the possibility of foreign missionary service. There was a great moving of the Spirit of God for the students to look to the world's fields which were "white already to harvest."[52] "The flood-tide of missionary enthusiasm had reached the universities."[53]

The Potential for the Service of God
In 1827, William Orne wrote,

> Few things in the history of religion are more interesting than the commencement and progress of Christianity on a young, an ardent, and a highly-cultivated mind. . . . It presents to such an individual a new world, teeming with objects of intense interest, and calling forth his deepest sympathy, and his noblest ambition.[54]

And indeed, since the days of the Reformation, nearly every major awakening or missionary movement can be traced to a college campus where professors and students were stirred by the Spirit of God. In addition, the historical development of campus ministries has influenced Bible translations in English and in other languages, the development of theological thinking including the roots of separatism, the vision for starting new Bible colleges, and the burden to evangelize the student body as well as the world.

---

[51]Courtney Anderson, *To the Golden Shore* (Valley Forge, PA: Judson Press, 1989), 50.

[52]John 4:35.

[53]Piggin and Roxborogh, *The St. Andrews Seven*, 43.

[54]Ibid., 12.

The need today is for campus ministries to be based out of the local church, with campus ministers unceasingly being occupied with the primacy of preaching the Word of God and the preeminence of Christ and His righteousness. The need is to pray that "the Lord of the harvest will send forth laborers"[55] to the campuses of America.

---

[55]Matt. 10:38.

3

THE PRESENT CULTURE OF THE SECULAR COLLEGE CAMPUS

ACADEMIC-ISMS ON THE SECULAR CAMPUS

To understand the campus ministry, one must understand the culture of the secular campus. Culture is the totality of socially transmitted patterns, arts, beliefs, and institutions, and all other products of human work and thought characteristic of a community or population.[1] In many ways, the campus ministry deals with a unique culture that is quite challenging to bridge and to understand. First, when one thinks of today's colleges, one immediately thinks of a place of higher education and of knowledge. But what actually is being taught on campuses today? The answer to this question can be generally summarized in one word: humanism.

Humanism is both a philosophy and a religion. The humanist's motto is "No deity will save us! We must save ourselves,"[2] and the first tenet of humanism is to present the theory of evolution as scientific fact and to recommend atheism or agnosticism as the religion of choice.

Today the public educational system is "dumbing down" society, attacking absolutes and standards, and advocating tolerance, in lieu of truth, as the greatest virtue of education. Tolerance of error has always preceded the rejection of truth. Postmodernism opposes

---

[1]Guenter Salter, *Isms that Disturb: Humanism, Multiculturalism and Postmodernism*, Bob Jones University Pastors' Fellowship, Columbia, SC, 2000.

[2]First tenet of *The Humanist Manifesto II* (Buffalo: Prometheus Books, 1973).

the biblical attributes of truth: eternal, immutable, indivisible, and absolute.

Secular colleges teach the theory of evolution in their science classes (e.g., chemistry, biology, astronomy, geology, physics). Many English literature classes feature pornographic and sensual materials. In the political science classes, the liberal position is advocated, and "Bill Clintons" are actively being cloned. In the psychology, sociology, psychiatry, and social science classes, professors present id, ego, super ego; Freud; Rogers; self-esteem; and New Age doctrines in an integrated fashion. The history classes ignore spiritual cause-and-effect relationships and the centrality of God in history while at the same time writing a pseudo-history. Philosophy and religion classes teach German rationalism, deny the inerrancy of the Bible, mock fundamentalism, and undermine what faith in God might be left in the students. The testimony of one Christian student attending a secular college summarizes the current situation: "Through biology I lost my faith in creation; through religion I lost my faith in the Bible; through sociology I lost my faith in the family; through psychology I lost my view of the depravity of man; and through philosophy I lost my faith in God."[3]

POLITICAL-ISMS ON THE SECULAR CAMPUS

Of the political and economic systems being taught, socialism and communism have received far more attention than capitalism. In many cases, capitalism is viewed as America's problem. With professors espousing such viewpoints, many students find it difficult to express their own political views in class or on their exams because of fear of losing academic standing because they have not taken the politically correct viewpoint. Fifteen percent of the professors of private and public schools state that they are politically conservative. Twenty-nine percent of those ages 18 to 24 consider themselves to be conservative. In the 2000 presidential election eighty-four percent of Ivy League professors voted for Al Gore, nine percent voted

---

[3]The Ivy Jungle Network, "The Campus Ministry Update," November 2000.

for George Bush, six percent for Ralph Nader.[4] The political goal of the world's colleges is, not surprisingly, globalism and a one-world government. The economic goal is similar: to have a one-world system and currency.[5]

In the 1960s the total budget for all colleges and universities was approximately $7 billion; in the early 1990s, it had surpassed $170 billion.[6] The reason for the increase was massive state and federal funding. The government wants to keep the colleges afloat financially to promote their agenda and to train future leaders. Spiritually speaking, Satan loves the college campus as his vehicle of infiltration and uses it to present his agenda "ye shall be as gods"[7] (humanism). In many ways, government funding is destroying higher education in America. George Roche, past president of Hillsdale College, states, "If I have learned anything at all in my career as an educator, it is this: Whom the gods would destroy, they first subsidize."[8] "Secular education in America is morally bankrupt, but it is quite literally going bankrupt."[9] Defaults on student loans have exploded. The annual default amount on the Stafford Loan is almost three billion dollars. Loan defaults and mismanagement cause much of the financial woes. More than six million government school loans are given each year. Nearly two-thirds of the undergraduate students at Harvard University receive financial aid. Tuition covers only one-quarter to one-third of the total school expenses of state schools. Private institutions are slightly higher, with tuition covering one-half to two-thirds of the school's actual expense for the student. This is a substantial amount of subsidizing when one recognizes that the average tuition cost of the private college in 2000 was $22,500.

---

[4]Bruce Bartlett, "Conservative Students Versus Their Faculty," September 11, 2003, http://townhall.com/columnists/BruceBartlett/2003/09/11/conservative_students_versus_their_faculty.

[5]Countering such anti-American views are the writings of political scientist Charles Dunn (i.e., *American Conservatism from Burke to Bush, American Political Theology, Conservative Tradition in America, Religion in American Politics*).

[6]George Roche, "How Government Funding Is Destroying Higher Education," *Imprimis*, October 1994, 10.

[7]Gen. 3:5.

[8]Roche, "Government Funding," 10.

[9]Ibid.

Government has thrown an enormous amount of money at higher education and has produced only lower morality. Michigan State University, which receives more than $230 million a year from the state treasury, says it needs millions more in government aid to "face the teaching challenges of the future."[10] America has stooped so low that it now seeks to fund education through lawful gambling and lotteries. This is one great step for organized crime, one giant leap backwards in education.

ETHNIC-ISMS ON THE SECULAR CAMPUS

Depending on the regional location of the college, the student body will typically have some dominant minority group. For example, on the West Coast one can expect a strong Asian influence on the campus. In the Southeast, one might expect the dominant minority group to be black Americans. Most academic subjects will be presented through the prism of gender and race oppression, where most groups are entitled to claim minority status as victims, except white males and Christians. Reverse discrimination in admissions, grading and employment will at times be noticed.

Special emphasis is often given to February as Black History month. One often senses a reverse discrimination during such times. This is a month to parade and march around the campus, celebrating the "dream" of Martin Luther King Jr. This is a part of the culture that may be foreign to some. Especially complicating this picture is the addition of black Muslims, who follow a modified Muslim creed to fit the culture of America. The goal to muslimize black Americans on campuses is very strong. Films such as *Malcolm X* introduce Muslim ideas to black audiences, which are often promoted by converted black athletes with names such as Mohammed, Ali, Rashad, Ishmael, Kareem, and Abdul. Islam expert Raymond Bakke explains Islam's appeal to the blacks: "It offers black men a brotherhood. They offer hope: a new name, wife, job. It's an integrated evangelistic strategy to replace the white man's gospel."[11]

---

[10]Ibid.

[11]The Ivy Jungle Network, "The Campus Ministry Update," November 2000.

There will be Hindus and Buddhists and other world religions represented on the campus, but there is no doubt that great advances are being made for Allah and Mohammed his prophet on the campus. This does not mean that someone will not encounter the culture of black gospel singing groups on campus. It is not uncommon to hear such groups singing their soul-stirring gospel songs. They may also use a new translation of the Bible produced by the African American Family Press called the *Black Bible Chronicles*. In translating the Ten Commandments, this version says, "You shouldn't diss the Almighty's name, using it in cuss words or rapping with one another. It ain't cool, and paycheck's a monster."[12] Another sample from the *Chronicles* is God's message to Noah: "I'm fed up with what's happening anymore, so I'm gonna do what I gotta do, and end things once and for all. Man, I'm gonna blow the brothers clear outta the water."[13]

According to the American Council of Education, two out of three African-American males who enroll in college do not graduate within six years. Across the nation, the six-year graduation rate for undergraduates is fifty-six percent, for black students it drops to forty percent and for black males to thirty-four percent.[14]

FEMINISM ON THE SECULAR CAMPUS

Sixty percent of the students enrolled on our 3,300 campuses are women.[15] Only one of the nation's 117 historically black colleges and universities has a majority of men (Morehouse College in Atlanta). Sixty-three percent of African-American undergraduates are women. This huge gender gap on the campuses may mean good news for the male student, but it also gives feminism a larger audience. Students must be prepared to hear a steady diet of feminism and new role models for women. The role of wife and mother and the high calling

---

[12]P. K. McCary and Andrew Young, *Black Bible Chronicles* (Houston: African American Family Press, 1995).

[13]Ibid.

[14]"A New Gender Gap," *U.S. News and World Report*, 8 February 1999, 46.

[15]Ibid.

of being "keepers at home"[16] will be minimized at best and will often be sneered at. The professional career woman who can play hardball is esteemed. Feminism presents a world conspiracy against women, and all men are guilty, both individually and collectively. As Phyllis Schlafly noted in a column entitled "Survival Message for College Students" on August 29, 2001, "At the University of California-Davis, law review policy is to use the female pronoun as a matter of course, except when referring to a criminal defendant, when a male pronoun is preferred."[17] She also notes that "at Arizona State University, drama professor Jared Sakren was fired for producing Shakespeare's 'Taming of the Shrew.'"[18] Obviously, Shakespeare is not politically correct. Harvard University offers a class called "Feminist Biblical Interpretation."

HEDONISM ON THE SECULAR CAMPUS

Homosexuality

College and university housing officials across the United States are implementing formal policies to force students and professors to accept the homosexual lifestyle as legitimate. Penn State University now has a formal policy that forbids freshmen from refusing to live with a homosexual roommate. According to the University, the new policy is to "shape attitudes about students who are different by virtue of race, ethnicity, or sexual orientation."[19] Three colleges of the University of California at Santa Cruz force all freshmen to attend "homophobia and bi-phobia" workshops.[20] A Stanford University official allows homosexual couples to use campus housing previously reserved for families.[21] The University of Oregon's housing units are open to homosexual couples who adopt children.[22] A student at the

---

[16]Titus 2:5.

[17]Phyllis Schlafly, "Survival Message for College Students," August 29, 2001, http://www.eagleforum.org/column/2001/aug01/01-08-29.shtml.

[18]Ibid.

[19]The Ivy Jungle Network, "The Campus Ministry Update," November 2000.

[20]Ibid.

[21]Ibid.

[22]Ibid.

University of Michigan who complained about a homosexual room-mate was described as "homophobic."[23] Practically every major college hosts a Lambda Society, an organization for homosexual students. In 2002, Southern Methodist University offered medical benefits and reduced tuition to the same-sex partners of employees.[24] This fact illustrates how much the homosexual agenda has advanced. Nationally, about 150 of the 3,300 higher education institutions offer similar policies, but Southern Methodist University is one of the first religious schools to offer such benefits. At some colleges, scholarships are now being offered to students who identify themselves as "other than heterosexual"; for example, Weber State University offers a $2,000 Matthew Shepherd Scholarship for such students.[25] Tufts University temporarily banned a chapter of InterVarsity from its campus for not allowing a lesbian student to run for a senior leadership position in the organization.

Pornography

Students attending a secular college must be prepared to see a barrage of pornography on the walls of the dormitory and to be introduced to seedy and sexual literature in their classes. Princeton University featured an eleven-week series of X-rated pornographic film clips, funded by the dean of students, the Woodrow Wilson School, the Council for Humanities, and six Princeton academic departments. There was standing room only, with five hundred students enrolled in the series.[26] Princeton University is perhaps the "porn prince" of the universities. Princeton's president, Harold Shapiro, recently appointed bio-ethicist Peter Singer as DeCamp Professor in the University Center for Human Values. Singer is in favor of euthanasia and moral relativism and smiles at bestiality.[27] Singer has previously equated killing disabled children with killing

---

[23]Ibid.

[24]"The Buzz: Deviance Pays," *World Magazine*, Volume 15, Number 49, (December 16, 2000), 7.

[25]Ibid.

[26]Ibid.

[27]Intercollegiate Studies Institute, "The 2001 Polly Award Winners," April 1, 2001, http://www.cnsnews.com/ViewCulture.asp?Page=\Culture\archive\200104\CUL20010401a.html.

animals and wrote a positive review of Midas Dekkers' book on bestiality, called *Dearest Pet: On Bestiality*. He argues that to kill animals for food is unjustifiable suffering. Ironically, he teaches that if humans are suffering then abortion, painless infanticide or euthanasia is justifiable.[28]

Immorality

Immorality is a way of life for many during their college days; students want sex without strings and relationships without rings. To encourage such a lifestyle, safe sex is taught, and free condoms are issued at the health centers on many college campuses. Despite such "benefits," there are still many communicable diseases being transmitted and unwanted pregnancies, which should not be surprising as college surveys record that fifty-seven percent of all collegians are sexually active.[29] At Clemson University alone there is a minimum of 300 abortions a year.[30] Many college-aged men and women, when surveyed by the National Marriage Project at Rutgers University, considered their career goals and buying a house more important than marriage and considered marriage a financial risk because of the high cost of divorce.[31]

Rock-and-Roll Music

Just as blue jeans are the universal uniform for college students, so rock-and-roll is their national anthem. Music plays a large part in dorm life. Some students like to share their music at all times with those on their hall or in their dormitory. Rock concerts are often held on the college campus in their gymnasiums or in their football stadiums and can be heard by the community several miles away.

On most campuses over the years, the emphasis has shifted from academic pursuits to having a good time. The culture of most universities promotes (not in written form or in their mission statements but in reality) partying and then studies. In some cases, colleges

---

[28]Wikipedia, "Abortion, Euthanasia and Infanticide," http://en.wikipedia.org/wiki/Peter_Singer, March 25, 2004, 1.

[29]The Ivy Jungle Network, "The Campus Ministry Update," November 2000.

[30]Elaine Davis, interview by William J. Senn III, January 1990.

[31]The Ivy Jungle Network, "The Campus Ministry Update," November 2000.

have very low standards for admission (e.g., Baker College, Fort Hays State University, and the College of West Virginia accept 100 percent of their applicants).[32] Most undergraduate students are pre-occupied with having a good time. This shift to hedonism is not only frustrating for the professors who want to teach such a group, but also makes it increasingly difficult to reach them with the gospel. Such hedonism is now not simply a student problem; it is an increasing problem amongst the faculty and administration. "The average professor in America now is in class only six to nine hours a week. At the University of Michigan, some professors teach so little that it is estimated that they make nearly $1000 an hour for their actual contact with students. In the last few years, teaching assistants, rather than faculty, have taught twenty-five, fifty, or even seventy-five percent of all introductory classes at schools such as Princeton University, the University of North Carolina, Ohio State University, Stanford University, and the University of California-Berkeley."[33] Going beyond hedonism is State University of New York (SUNY)-Albany's new campus club called the Power Exchange, which is New York's first sadomasochism club. A SUNY university official summarizes the official attitude toward Power Exchange: "As long as they abide by the student guidelines, they have a right to have their club officially recognized by the student association on campus and to be funded by the student association."[34]

Alcohol and Drugs

According to a recent Core Institute study of approximately 50,000 representative college students, twenty percent reported drinking three or more times per week.[35] Thirty-eight percent reported having engaged in binge drinking in the previous two weeks. Twenty-two percent reported that they performed poorly on a test or projects due to alcohol usage. Twenty-eight percent reported that they

---

[32]Ibid.

[33]Roche, "Government Funding," 10.

[34]CNSNews.com, "Group 'Honors' Campus P.C. Extremists," NewsMax.com, April 3, 2001, http://archive.newsmax.com/archives/articles/2001/4/2/202952.shtml.

[35]The Ivy Jungle Network, "The Campus Ministry Update," November 2000.

had missed classes, twenty-six percent reported that they had experienced memory loss, thirty percent became embroiled in an argument or a fight, forty-seven percent reported nausea or vomiting, fourteen percent reported being hurt or injured, and thirty-three percent reported driving under the influence. Today, college administrations are marketing moderation; twenty-one national higher education associations banned the term "binge drinking" as inaccurate and counterproductive, hoping to market moderation as the thing that everyone else is doing. Police captain Dale Burke of the University of Wisconsin says that alcohol is the "number one problem on every college campus in this country."[36] University of Wisconsin's Madison campus led the nation with 792 alcohol violations in 1998. Michigan State came in second with 655. In 2002, the top ten party schools based on a survey of 100,158 students by *Princeton Review* are Indiana University of Bloomington, Clemson University, University of Alabama of Tuscaloosa, Penn State University, University of Florida, SUNY at Buffalo, University of New Hampshire, University of Colorado at Boulder, Florida State University and University of Wisconsin at Madison.[37]

Other Problems

Twenty-nine percent of college students smoke cigarettes in comparison to the twenty-five percent of the general public that smoke. The campus has become a dangerous place, not only morally but also otherwise when one notes the soaring crime rate on the campuses. In a survey of 580 campuses between 1990 and 1992 there were 2,528 assaults; 15,313 burglaries; 5,081 car thefts; 928 robberies; 493 reported rapes; and 16 murders.[38]

Sports at all levels are king on the campus. Sports programs typically run and fund the major universities and are big business. Coaches are paid hundreds of thousands of dollars. College athletic programs have now mutated into farm clubs for professional teams.

---

[36]Ibid.

[37]Robert Franek and Tom Meltzer, "The Best 345 Colleges: 2003 Edition— Top 20 Party School List," *The Princeton Review*, August 27, 2002, 43.

[38]The Ivy Jungle Network, "The Campus Ministry Update," November 2000.

Student athletes are awarded scholarships to play sports but often do not graduate or do not graduate on time (within four years).

Plagiarism and other forms of cheating at the college level are on the increase. *The American Family Physician* (1991) surveyed thirty-one of the "academically elite" colleges and found that sixty-seven percent of 6,000 students cheated at least once. Business majors cheated the most, with the engineering students a close second.[39] To learn how to cheat better, steal exams, and pass answers, there is an 87-page guide written by Michael Moore entitled *Cheating 101: The Benefits and Fundamentals of Earning the Easy A*.

SPIRITUAL-ISMS ON THE SECULAR CAMPUS

Liberalism

Many campuses were once orthodox in doctrine, revered the Bible, conducted daily chapels and were founded by born-again Christians. Over the years, the schools were surrendered into the hands of the unbelieving liberals. Many schools at one time had daily or weekly chapel services where the Bible was preached. Traces of the "good old days" can be seen on some of these campuses with buildings named after godly men and women. Today there are colleges that are still linked to some church or denomination, but these groups play an almost invisible role on the campus except for the church with the high steeple and few people. There will be some appeal to the students from the mainline churches in a college community. Often their churches are the closest to the campus. This visibly illustrates how at one time church and God were important to the administrations of both the school and the denomination. Easy accessibility to such impressive edifices traps some. Liberal Protestant denominations and Roman Catholics have their student organizations. The Catholics have their Newman Foundation; the Lutherans have their Lutheran Student Movement; the United Methodists have their Wesleyan Foundation; the Episcopalians have their Canterbury Foundation; the Baptists have their Baptist Student Union (ranging from liberal to conservative, depending on who is in control).

---

[39]Trudy Keyes, *The American Family Physician* [September 1991], 725.

Each college community will have a liberal ministerial association that will be given presence at social, cultural, and athletic events. Many colleges will tolerate the liberal clergy and often use these men for marketing the school to students and especially parents. Such clergy are asked to pray but are often asked not to use the name of Jesus in their prayer, for that would be going too far in the prayer and could be offensive. Clemson University has a "Public Prayer Policy" which reads, "Clemson University is a multicultural community and because students, faculty and staff are of many different religious persuasions, prayers given at University-sponsored public events should be nonsectarian."[40] The aim of the liberal clergyman and the university is to bring about a harmonious and peaceful relationship between the state college and church and to prepare the students for such peace at a global level, ideally a one-world church and government.

New Evangelicalism

Once the campuses were handed over to the liberals, a huge void was created on the campuses. During the last half of the twentieth century, parachurch organizations responded to the spiritual needs of the students. Some of these groups started off within the fundamentalist movement and then drifted into compromise. These groups are theologically neither hot nor cold, liberal or fundamentalist, but are contented middle-of-the-roaders. Such organizations greatly appeal to the student who comes from a church background because he can have his campus life as well as a taste of religious life that these groups offer. These organizations will often replace students' need to attend church. Most students are glad to be away from home with the only strings to home being mom's purse strings. Strong spiritual accountability is not the desire of many, so organizations that appeal to the flesh, yet are called Christian, fit their desires nicely.

Contemporary "Christian" rock music is one characteristic that ties all new evangelical campus organizations together. This is especially demonstrated when the campus groups work together to promote

---

[40] *Clemson University Student Handbook 2002–2003*, 93.

a local "Christian" rock concert or a dance. Another characteristic of such groups is that they downplay Bible doctrine, de-emphasize Bible words, and avoid teachings that might be divisive. The new evangelical emphasizes a "sloppy agape" and pursues a unity divorced from truth. The fundamentalist's view is that doctrinal error is not to be overlooked for "love" or for "unity." Speaking in tongues is a common topic for the new evangelical student to practice or to tolerate charitably within his organization. One who contends for the faith and emphasizes doctrinal integrity and moral purity is often seen as judgmental, narrow, and critical and will most certainly be called a "legalist." Typically, such new evangelical organizations are active politically and are willing to get involved in anti-abortion protests or political causes. They are often interested in reaching high school kids.

Most new evangelical campus groups have few or no ties to a local church and often view their organizations as superior to God's plan for this age, the local church. It does not bother them to plan meetings, services, and activities that compete with Sunday church services or Wednesday night prayer meetings. This attitude is seen in an article called "Students Dig Christ but Hate the Church." A Campus Crusade staff worker is quoted, saying, "We're not hoot and holler types and we don't push the kids to go to church. That's the last thing we do. . . . We tell them Christ was the greatest revolutionary that ever lived and He was the world's greatest non-conformist. That really perks up the kids' interest. They can identify with this kind of Christ."[41] The vocabulary may have changed since the 1960s, but the parachurch's prevailing attitude toward the local church has not. The leadership for such groups is often in the hands of the neophyte or the poorly trained; consequently much pride is often seen in the charismatic leader. The appeal and motivation for ministry is typically emotional rather than substantial. There is little stress placed on holiness or personal standards. The biblical doctrine of separation is a foreign concept. Inferior Bible translations are often used by the students as they pool their Bible

---

[41]"Students Dig Christ but Hate the Church," *Los Angeles Examiner*, March 25, 1969.

ignorance in their weekly rallies and paraphrase studies. The gospel is preached at times, and students are saved, but often the message does not include the doctrine of repentance. Instead an "easy-be-lievism" is presented without the need of a changed life. Again, those who stress a changed life and holiness are pegged "legalists." New evangelical groups that one could find on a college campus include InterVarsity, Navigators, Campus Crusade, Fellowship of Christian Athletes (FCA), International Christian Fellowship (ICF), Great Commission Students, Reformed University Fellowship (RUF), and International Students Christian Fellowship (ISCF).

The Cults
The cults are running rampant on college campuses. They have "wisely" targeted the secular campus as one of their primary re-cruiting grounds and are prepared, organized, funded, and aggres-sive. They offer a false hope and a fuzzy friendship to searching and lonely students. The Mormons (Latter-Day Saints) will be found chartered at most larger campuses, with their "elders" handing out *The Book of Mormon* and other literature. The Church of Christ has its Theophilus Club. The Jehovah's Witnesses are also seeking to add to their numbers. With typically little or no representation of fundamentalists on the secular campus, the cults are generally un-checked and unchallenged.

Occultism
Satanism is on the rise on secular campuses. On some campuses there are clubs, such as the Dungeons and Dragons club and or-ganizations that teach the occult. "Joe Freshman" needs to be pre-pared to see the remains of animals on campus that were sacrificed on certain unholy days. Some schools actually offer classes on the occult.[42]

The New Age movement is gaining popularity on secular campuses as well. The Oak Grove campus organization, which is chartered at the University of New Mexico, Ohio State University, the University of Massachusetts, MIT, and the University of Washington,

[42]The Ivy Jungle Network, "The Campus Ministry Update," November 2000.

advertises that "most of us believe in reincarnation. We see the god and goddess in everything. Only a Christian can be a Satanist; we don't believe in their God or their Satan."[43]

Over four hundred years ago Martin Luther expressed his fears of education divorced from God. He said, "I am much afraid that the universities will prove to be the great gates to Hell, unless they diligently labour to explain the Holy Scriptures and to engrave them upon the hearts of youth. I advise no one to place his child where the Scriptures do not reign paramount. Every institution where men are not unceasingly occupied with the Word of God must become corrupt."[44]

Fundamentalism
Sadly, fundamentalism has abandoned the secular campus. Actually there are several local churches and fundamental mission boards that have a burden for reaching collegians for Christ, but their campus presence is minimal. Their missionary efforts are typically poorly supported, limiting fundamentalists to very few full-time campus workers. Although the campus-ministry movement believes in the local church, the campus ministry generally has little support from the local church and minimal interaction and involvement with it. Due to the fundamentalists' strong conviction regarding Christian education, the emphasis of churches has rightly been on Christian colleges for the training of their own flocks. However, in the process, the movement has lost sight of the mission field of the secular college campus. As a whole, the movement has turned the campus over to the liberals, the cults, the occult, and the new evangelicals. This neglect is one reason for this book: the need for the fundamentalist to regain the vision of reaching collegians for Christ. There is no question that Satan does not want fundamentalists on the campus and has worked hard to remove their presence through discouragement and compromise. Most secular colleges will tolerate practically any philosophy except fundamentalism. A leading periodical for secular educators is *The Chronicle of Higher*

---

[43]Keyes, *The American Family Physician* [September 1991]: 725.
[44]Tan, *Illustrations*, 159.

Education. In 1989 they warned their academic peers that "cult-like methods are being used by Christian Fundamentalist groups."[45] The article argues that the secular university has the "responsibility to protect minds from being raped by groups [fundamentalists] that are unethical and using college campuses for recruiting."[46] The article states that the students who join a fundamentalist group are the same ones "who in earlier years might have joined such groups as the Hare Krishnas or the Unification Church."[47]

To have the most effective ministry on the secular campus, the campus worker needs to have some knowledge of the multi-dimensioned culture of the secular campus. Indeed, it is in many ways a foreign culture within the American culture. The fundamentalist has an uphill battle to achieve a presence on the secular campus, but history has demonstrated repeatedly that God's Spirit is able. Indeed, the campus ministry will be accomplished not by fundamentalists' "might, nor by power,"[48] but by God's Spirit.

[45]Tanya Gazdik, "Some Colleges Warn Students that Cult-Like Methods Are Being Used by Christian Fundamentalist Groups," *The Chronicle of Higher Education*, November 15, 1989, 1.

[46]Ibid., 42.

[47]Ibid.

[48]Zech. 4:6.

4

THE ORGANIZATIONAL MODELS TO REACH THE CAMPUS

The organizational key for the fundamentalist is to determine which model to follow in reaching the secular campus. By first studying the historic models for reaching collegians on the campus, the fundamentalist can incorporate the lessons learned from history and develop better models for reaching the secular campus based on a clear goal.

THE HISTORIC MODELS IN REACHING COLLEGIANS

Ironically, many of the colleges that are now mission fields once biblically trained missionaries. For example, at one time Harvard, Yale, and Princeton were fundamentally sound Bible colleges. Puritans, Congregationalists, and separatists from the Presbyterian and Baptist movements sent their students to these colleges with the utmost confidence that their young people would be strengthened in the faith and further equipped and sharpened for Christian service. The relationship between the Bible-believing church and the college was complementary.

The Fundamental Christian College Model

Bible-believing churches sending students to Bible-believing colleges	Bible-believing colleges training students to serve in Bible-believing ministries	Students graduating to minister in Bible-believing churches

Over time, many of the Bible colleges "tolerated" error, compromise, and infiltration of unbelief; consequently, the Bible colleges ran aground. However, at first the denominations and churches did not cease to send their students to such schools. The result was the following model:

Bible-believing churches sending students to compromising and apostate colleges	Compromising and apostate colleges training students to be compromisers and infidels	Compromisers and unbelievers graduating to minister in Bible-believing churches

What happened next is quite easy to see. When the Bible colleges went liberal, they trained a generation of leaders to be liberal. As a result, the churches that once believed the Bible were being led subsequently by liberal ministers. This situation created a real dilemma in the mainline denominations: first their colleges had gone liberal, and now their churches had. These churches still had born-again Christians in them; some of these Christians would compromise and stay in, while others would adhere to the principles of biblical separation and "come out."[1] During this transition, which ultimately came to its head in the Modernist-Fundamentalist Controversy of the 1920s, there were spiritually struggling students on America's campuses. There was a push, mostly by the conservative element of the mainline denominations, to reach them and to provide some spiritual respite for them while they were at college. The solution was to create foundations, which typically adjoined the campus, where the students could congregate, fellowship, and be spiritually encouraged. The first of these foundations was founded at the University of Illinois in 1907.[2]

The Foundation Model

Bible-believing and apostate churches sending students to apostate colleges	Infidels training students	Conservative denominational foundations ministering to students	Students graduating confused and attending either conservative or liberal churches

During the first half of the 1900s, the denominations were warring, the churches were being divided, mankind faced two world wars,

---

[1]2 Cor. 6:17.

[2]Stacey Wood, *The Growth of a Work of God* (Downers Grove, IL: InterVarsity, 1978), 15.

and America went through a depression. It was no doubt a time of turmoil and transition. In the 1920s new Bible colleges were emerging, such as Westminster Theological Seminary and Bob Jones College; however, the "modernists" (liberals) were gaining control of the mainline denominations, with their greatest accomplishment being the formation of the World Council of Churches in 1948. They also gained control of the campus foundations. Then the campus ministry model looked like this:

Apostate churches sending students to apostate colleges	Infidels training students	Apostate foundations ministering to students	Students graduating as infidels with a majority of them attending apostate churches or being disillusioned with church

As a result, a tremendous void for truth was found on the campuses of America. There was a huge vacuum on the college campus for Bible Christianity and the gospel. As a result of this incredible need, the campus parachurch movement was born in America in the 1940s. Leading the way to minister the gospel to the students was InterVarsity, then the Navigators, and then Campus Crusade. These three organizations pioneered campus ministry but had no ties to the local church or to a denomination. At first, each of these three groups was aligned to varying degrees with the fundamentalist movement. Now the campus-ministry model looked like this:

The Parachurch Model

Unchurched students going to college	Infidels training students	Parachurch organizations ministering to students	Saved students graduating with little instruction or loyalty to a Bible-believing church; unsaved student remaining unchurched

From the 1940s to the present, campus parachurch organizations have done the majority of the spiritual work on the college campuses. Unfortunately, they have had little or no accountability to the local church. They have given pre-eminence to building their organizations rather than to the church. Their loyalties lie with their parachurch organization. Tragically, most of these parachurch organizations have compromised the truth and are on the steep downgrade to denying the truth. The impending domino effect of the compromises of the campus parachurch organizations is poised to create another vacuum for truth on the campuses. This time who will fill the gap? In the past, when there was a spiritual void on the campus, there was a conservative response; unfortunately, each organizational response took campus ministry one step further away from a connection with the local church. Today, there are several fundamentalist ministries that are wisely viewing the secular campus as a mission field, which creates the following model:

The Missionary Model

Unchurched students going to college	Infidels training students	Campus missionaries working out of a local church ministering to students	Saved students graduating with a knowledge of the local church

Within the fundamentalist movement, Campus Bible Fellowship, Campus Light and several other mission boards are engaged in reaching college students with the gospel. Such ministries present the secular campus as a mission field just as they would a foreign field. The campus worker bases his ministry out of a local church near the campus. He will have responsibilities to his mission board, supporting churches (20 to 100 churches), and his local church. At times these relationships are difficult to maintain, and on some occasions, the many roles and relationships will create irreconcilable conflicts between different parties. The question of loyalties is raised: mission board first or local church first? This model is superior to the parachurch model but is not without its organizational challenges and relational gymnastics.

The ultimate model, in the author's estimation, is for churches in large college towns (more than 5,000 students) to have a goal of having a campus pastor on the church staff whose primary ministry is the mission field of the secular campus. His role would be to see the saved students involved in the local church. This model should be the goal of every fundamental church in a large college town.

The Campus Pastor Model

Unchurched students going to college	Infidels training students	Campus pastor of a local church ministering to students	Saved students graduating with a deep appreciation for and loyalty to the local church

However, in many cases, this goal may be unrealistic for many reasons, such as lack of finances for the local church to hire a full-time staff worker for the campus ministry. What then should a local church consider? One answer is for the church to go back to the missionary model and seek to have a mission board supply a missionary who would be based out of that church. Another solution is to combine the campus pastor and the missionary models as presented below.

The Campus Pastor/Missionary Model

Unchurched students going to college	Infidels training students	Campus missionary, who is on the staff of the local church, ministering to students	Saved students graduating with a deep appreciation for and loyalty to the local church

In the history of campus ministry, this particular model has been illustrated by accident but never by design. This model presents the missionary as a pastoral staff member of the local church. The local church takes on as much support as possible, with the majority of the remaining support coming from the churches within that state. The long-term goal is for the local church of the campus pastor/missionary to fully support the office of the campus pastor. This approach parallels that of a church-planting project where the new church is ultimately self-supporting. From the beginning, this would be the goal communicated to all parties. The missionary's organizational loyalty would be first to the local church and then to the mission agency assisting in the project. The mechanics of this model are articulated in chapters eleven through thirteen.

Because most college-town churches are not able to fund a full-time campus pastor, this model gives the local church a good alternative. The only fundamental campus mission board that follows this model is Cross Impact Ministries, formerly called the Spurgeon

Foundation Campus Ministries, which will be used as an example throughout this manual.

Before starting a campus ministry on a secular campus, the leadership of the local church should weigh out the advantages and the disadvantages of each of the above models and decide on an organizational strategy suited to their particular needs. There is something to learn both positively and negatively from each model. The advantages and disadvantages of each model are as follows:

The Advantages and Disadvantages of the Foundation Model

THE ADVANTAGES	THE DISADVANTAGES
1. For an established church in the same college town, a foundation could be a great investment to add another dimension to their outreach.	1. There is only a distant relationship to the local church if the foundation is solely a satellite building in the college town.
2. The foundation's building could be used for counseling purposes and outreach.	2. It is very expensive to purchase or rent a building to establish a haven of rest near the campus.
3. The foundation could provide more campus presence for the church if it is clearly identified and associated with the church.	
4. The foundation building could be a dormitory building for Christian students and be used as an outreach post.	

The Advantages and the Disadvantages of the Parachurch Model

The Advantages	The Disadvantages
1. The local church has minimal to no financial commitment.	1. There is little or no commitment to the local church.
2. The church is able to focus on ministries other than campus work.	2. Loyalty is to organization before the church.
	3. If students even attend church, they can be removed from the church at the whim of the leader-ship of the parachurch organization because the students are "their" converts.
	4. There is potential competition between the church and the parachurch organization, particularly with odd possessiveness of converts.
	5. Separation issues flaw the entire parachurch campus ministry movement.
	6. Doctrinal differences could forbid an official alliance with such groups.

The Advantages and the Disadvantages of the Missionary Model

THE ADVANTAGES	THE DISADVANTAGES
1. There are several good mission boards to serve with.	1. Churches do not have much interest in supporting a campus missionary, especially if his ministry is in another state.
2. It is a viable approach to reaching the campus.	2. The missionary has many relationships to maintain: mission board, supporting churches, and home church of the ministry.
3. The missionary status stresses the true nature of the campus as a mission field.	3. There are possible conflicts between the goals and philosophy of the local church and those of the mission board.
4. The missionary has additional sources of counsel with both mission board and home church.	4. The missionary never feels fully a part of the local church's ministry.
	5. Potentially, the missionary may not be involved in the leadership meetings of the church.
	6. The need of reporting to all the supporting churches from time to time removes the missionary from the campus.
	7. The missionary lacks flexibility to do other aspects of ministry with the local church beyond the scope of campus ministry.
	8. The missionary could change churches, and the former local church could lose most of its campus ministry as the college students follow the missionary.

The Advantages and the Disadvantages of the Campus Pastor/Missionary Model

THE ADVANTAGES	THE DISADVANTAGES
1. Clear lines of loyalties are drawn.	1. All parties must clearly understand and communicate the goals of this model.
2. A worker is provided for the campus mission field.	2. The campus worker needs to do some deputation work at first and to follow up with the necessary correspondence and visits.
3. A state-wide awareness is presented to reach all the major campuses in the state.	3. Some people overlook the missionary nature of the office and believe that the local church has a staff worker who is being paid for by other churches.
4. A network of communication is created within the state to pass on names of students to follow up with on the campus.	
5. The campus worker is involved in all of the leadership meetings and structure of the church.	
6. He is able to tackle other ministries in the church proportionate to the financial support of the local church.	
7. It gives the local church a goal and a push to finance another staff position.	

The Advantages and the Disadvantages of the Campus Pastor Model

THE ADVANTAGES	THE DISADVANTAGES
1. The campus pastor does not have to be accountable to multiple organizations; he is directly responsible to the local church.	1. The local church may not be able to fund such a position immediately
2. The campus pastor is involved in the leadership meetings of the local church.	2. The local church may not have the vision to fund such a position.
3. The campus pastor reaps the benefits of not needing to report to or visit supporting churches.	
4. He is able to involve students in the various aspects of the local church.	
5. Because his income comes from church, the campus pastor could do other tasks within the ministry when needs surface.	
6. The campus pastor can have multiple ministries to oversee; however, in a large college town the campus pastor eventually does not need to wear too many hats as the campus ministry alone is more than a full-time need.	

This manual has not discussed the senior pastor doing the primary work of the campus ministry because he will quickly realize his own limitations on the campus, especially as it relates to the time demands of the campus ministry. Another model that has not been mentioned is the campus layman model. In this model, a layman in the church oversees the campus ministry. This person could be the college/career Sunday school teacher or a layman in the church, an extension worker, an intern, or a retired missionary. At first the lay leader would work with the college/career Sunday school class as the main organizational vehicle to minister to college students.

The Advantages and the Disadvantages of the Campus Layman Model

The Advantages	The Disadvantages
1. A part-time worker doing some campus work is better than no one doing campus work.	1. Typically the campus layman does not have much time to give to campus ministry. When a church borders a large campus, there is abundant work to be done.
2. It is a starting point.	
3. It can buy time for the local church to increase its vision and burden for campus ministry.	2. There will most likely be minimal campus presence from the church.
4. It can confirm the need for a full-time campus worker.	
5. It will benefit the workers involved and will cause them to grow.	
6. There is minimal staff expense.	
7. It will provide the church staff and church family greater insight as to the challenges of the campus ministry. They will understand better the future campus pastor's or missionaries' role.	

To start a campus ministry, the local church must prayerfully determine which model best fits their goals and ministries. The church's selection is then placed in block three of the following organizational chart.

The Campus Ministry Organizational Chart for the Local Church

1. The Lord Jesus Christ as the Head of the Church

2. The Senior Pastor as the Under-Shepherd of the Church

3. Selection of Leadership Model: layman, added responsibility given to a present, pastoral staff member, missionary, campus missionary, or campus pastor

4. College/Career Class Teacher   5. Faculty/Staff Advisor   6. Student Officers

7. University students doing "the work of the ministry" (Eph. 4:12)

It may seem like there is "too much string on the kite," but as one gives it some time, it will fly. The role of the pastor as the under-shepherd and overseer is to define the mission statement, ministry goals, and guidelines for workers and to give the job description for each of the organization's leaders. He is to establish clear lines of communication and periodic meetings or checkpoints (weekly is suggested) to discuss the needs and progress of the work. The pastor is the macro-manager who sets the direction for the campus ministry.

The director of the campus ministry, whether he be a layman, present staff worker, missionary, or campus pastor, does the micromanaging, the hands-on work of the campus ministry. His goal is to implement the specifics of the mission statement and to oversee and coordinate the many details of the campus ministry. The campus worker, if not the college/career Sunday school teacher, needs to coordinate the campus work with the teacher of that class. There needs to be input at this level and a clear understanding of the goals and game plan as the Sunday school class will play an integral part of the goals of the local church's campus ministry. The faculty advisor, which is a position required by the secular college for chartering purposes, should be included in the campus ministry and regularly informed and consulted as to the details of the campus calendar and ministry and occasionally asked to speak to the students at one of the meetings.

The student officers are the cavalry of the campus ministry, doing much of the actual leg work for the organization. They will be invaluable in giving input and implementing the goals for the activities, fellowships, programs, advertising, promotions, and rallies. Ultimately the growing campus ministry will have its students doing "the work of the ministry." It will be this group who will have the natural contacts with fellow students and can become an army of soulwinners and disciplers. The true strength of a college ministry is seen at this level and will reflect on the leadership at all levels. As the local church's ministry grows, other tiers may be added under the campus worker on the leadership chart above, such as extension workers, interns, lady staff workers, or an international pastor.

Once the organizational model has been prayerfully selected, it will be extremely important to formulate the church's philosophy and goals for its campus ministry and the people and the tools needed to get the job done.

There is no question for the Bible-believing local church that the aim is to fulfill the Great Commission. This goal should be at the heart of the campus ministry: to make disciples, to baptize the converts, and to teach "them to observe all things" (Matthew 28:19–20). A clear mission statement is needed to keep the focus of campus ministry on track. The following is an example of the mission statement of the Cross Impact Ministries (formerly called Spurgeon Foundation Campus Ministries), which was adopted on June 23, 1997:

> The Mission Statement of Cross Impact Ministries: The mission of CIM is to reach college students with the gospel, disciple and train them to fulfill the Great Commission in Matthew 28:19–20 (which includes being baptized) and encourage them to take an active role in the local church by faithful attendance and participation in ministry.

In the process of establishing the specifics of such goals for the campus ministry, the local church can learn from the ministry models of the three oldest campus ministries in America.

THE MINISTRY MODEL OF INTERVARSITY

It should not be surprising that the first American parachurch campus ministry had its roots at Cambridge. In 1877 the Cambridge Inter-collegiate Christian Union came into existence as a result of the student revivals that took place between 1860 and 1880. Inter-Varsity was founded in 1919, when the question was raised to the Student Christian Movement, which had united with the Inter-collegiate Christian Union, was the atoning blood of Christ the central point of their message. When they responded that it was not, Inter-Varsity was born to preach the blood of Christ as the central point of their message. In the late 1920s Dr. Howard Guinness traveled to the University of Washington and began a campus ministry called University Christian Fellowship. Not much took place on this first effort to establish an Inter-Varsity chapter in America.

During this same time period others were burdened for campus ministry. One such individual was Dr. J. Gresham Machen, who had separated from the downgrade of Princeton Seminary and was involved in founding Westminster Seminary. He was burdened for America's student population and the growing effects of liberalism in the colleges. He saw the deadening effects of theological students attending liberal colleges and founded an organization called The League of Evangelical Students. His goal was to see spiritual graduate students salvage undergraduate students. Two things took place: the undergraduates wanted their own movement, and many of the graduate students tended to be hyper-Calvinistic or were not burdened for this project. Consequently the League died just as Guinness's efforts at the University of Washington had died.

In 1941 Dr. Guinness and Inter-Varsity had an impulse to try again to break ground in the United States. This time it was successful. On January 31, 1942, The Michigan Christian Fellowship was incorporated, and Inter-Varsity was truly born. Inter-Varsity then started ministries at Wayne State University, Swarthmore College, and the University of Pennsylvania and rapidly established chapters across America.

Over time InterVarsity has drifted from their central theme of preaching that Christ's blood atones for sin. They have quickly departed from a nominal evangelical position and have moved toward ecumenical heresy, charismatic error, psychological techniques, worldly worship, and New Age philosophies. The blood of Christ is no longer central. What led to this doctrinal decline? The answer is the lack of accountability to the local church and a broad doctrinal statement from the beginning. InterVarsity has no formal position on eschatology, baptism, church government, Calvinism, Arminianism, tongues-speaking, or other key doctrines. They have boasted that they are truly interdenominational, stating "Happily students coming from Seventh-Day Adventist churches and Pentecostal churches, to say nothing of the occasional Mormon or Christian Scientist, have found fellowship within our chapters."[3] Their motto is "All one in Christ."

---

[3]Ibid., 70.

The strengths of InterVarsity were their early interest to preach Christ and Him crucified; their emphasis on student initiative, involvement, and ownership in the campus ministry; their four-week training school for campus workers at Cedar Campus, Michigan; their student rallies at Urbana; their annual meetings; their apologetics materials; and their printing press. A weakness was that the leadership of InterVarsity would train student leaders and then turn the ministry loose to the students. Their failure is summarized by Clarence Shedd, church historian at Yale Divinity School: "Christian societies have flourished when students themselves have steered them, with adult advisors in reserve."[4] The result has been that they have "flourished" but have delegated too much to the neophyte, who often does not have the discernment to steer the organization into sound doctrine.

"The character of the summer leadership training program likewise changed. The quality of the teaching staff weakened. Leading theologians, apologists and Bible expositors were no longer widely used. Staff members themselves tended to take the place of these outside teachers. In spite of efforts to the contrary, straight Bible exposition largely went out the window, and weak inductive Bible study without personal application reigned. Staff took less leadership and did less direct counseling; they became more passive and waited for students to take the initiative to come to them. Student initiative and responsibility were emphasized too much and staff influence and leadership too little. The mood then was one of hesitation to impose one's conviction upon another, while permissive Christian liberty and antinomianism reached a disastrous peak. Regular quiet time, Bible reading and prayer were discouraged as legalistic."[5] InterVarsity would repudiate the biblical doctrine of separation.

InterVarsity regularly hosts the Urbana Student Missions Conference. During the conference held from December 27–31, 2003, 19,000 students and recent alumni attended their twentieth student conference.[6]

---

[4]Clarence Shedd, *The Church Follows Its Students* (New Haven: Yale University Press, 1938), 32.

[5]Ibid.

[6]"Urbana Student Missions Conference 2003," http://www.urbana.org/.

In 2000, InterVarsity had more than 1,000 staff serving more than 34,000 core students and faculty nation-wide.

The Ministry Model of Navigators

A young man nicknamed "Porky" was known as a chronic liar, an obsessive gambler, and a pool shark. He enjoyed his motorcycle and his sin. His mother said, "I can't believe a word he says." One night he found himself in jail. The word went out to "Pray for Dawson." Mrs. Lewis, a Pentecostal woman, had a vision of Dawson holding a Bible and speaking to many people. Not too many days later, Dawson Earle "Porky" Trotman attended a Christian Endeavor meeting in 1926 and was gloriously converted. He immediately began memorizing Scripture and winning souls in the Fisherman's Club. He read missionary biographies and woke up at 5:00 a.m. to pray. He read how D. L. Moody said, "God has yet to show what He can do through the life of a man who is wholly yielded to Him." Dawson said, "O God, let me be that man."

In 1928 he went to Biola College. After his first year, he dropped out of college, but not from his service of the Lord. He returned home and continued his involvement in winning souls on a bus route and was involved heavily with his Presbyterian church. The church called a new pastor, who was a liberal. Two of the revered Bible-believing Sunday school teachers were relieved of their teaching duties. As a result of this, Dawson left the church and started his own church. The first sermon he ever preached was on the "Seven Churches of Revelation." On the first day, 126 people showed up. Later he would regret the way he separated from the liberal church and would call it unwise. "I had failed to recognize that II Corinthians 6:17 applies to separation from unbelievers, not believers with whom you disagree."[7] This statement is consistent with his earlier understanding of the doctrine of separation. He wrote of Christian Endeavor (C. E.) in these words: "C. E. is being drawn into modernism. God must, it seems, provide something to take its place."[8] Navigators was

---

[7]Skinner, *DAWS*, 60.
[8]Ibid., 59.

started as a result of Trotman separating from C. E.'s compromises. Over the years, Trotman's view of biblical separation eroded. One reason for this was the counsel he often received from doctrinally weak Christian leaders. One such leader was Charles Fuller, who said to Dawson, "Don't you be critical of any under-shepherd God has placed in the pulpit. He may not have the gift of vision or knowledge you have, but *teach your men to cooperate.*"[9] Unfortunately, Trotman would "cooperate" with some men who were clearly disobedient to the Scriptures.

Dawson pioneered a boys club, which he called the Navigators. Later he started a ministry for servicemen that was first called "The Service Men's Bible Club." Later he called it the Navigators. This ministry would branch out to include a campus ministry that at one time was the Marines of campus ministries. The old Navigators knew the Word.

On one occasion Dawson was praying and asked the Lord for an idea to easily communicate the gospel and the Christian life. The Lord, Dawson said, "gave [him] the idea" of the wheel to illustrate the Christian life. From the object lesson of the wheel came a topical Bible memory program. Later he added other devotional tools such as the "Log," a devotional checklist.

The motto of Navigators is "To Know Christ and To Make Him Known." The strength of the older Navigators ministry was its solid discipleship material and the emphasis on biblical discipleship. The young Billy Graham used the Navigators' materials in his earlier years of ministry when he preached the gospel and was concerned with his converts being discipled biblically and involved in a Bible-believing church. The Navigators was a fundamental ministry for years. In 1950 Trotman was looking for area representatives for Navigators. He stated he was looking for "top-notchers." At Bob Jones University alone in one year he recruited over 400 "top-notchers." In 1956 Trotman drowned while trying to save a girl's life at Schroon Lake, New York, at the Word of Life Christian camp and conference center.

_____
[9]Ibid.

The weaknesses of Navigators are seen in what is omitted in their discipleship materials: biblical teaching on the local church and biblical separation. As a result of these two weaknesses, Navigators, like InterVarsity, has compromised the truth and has been theologically drifting for years.

THE MINISTRY MODEL OF CAMPUS CRUSADE

A man greatly influenced by Dawson Trotman and who also had a burden for campus ministries was Bill Bright. He attended Fuller Seminary and dropped out of college his senior year to "obey God's heavenly vision" to reach college campuses with the gospel. He sought advice from Dr. Wilbur Smith, Billy Graham, Dawson Trotman, Dan Fuller, and Edwin Orr about the prospects of a campus ministry. He then established a 24-hour prayer chain and divided it into 96 periods of 15-minute prayer times. In 1951 he started a campus ministry at UCLA known as the "Little Red School House." In 1954 UCLA won the number one ranking in college football; nine out of the eleven starters on offense were Christians whom Bright had led to the Lord. He had over 250 converts in his first years on the campus. One of the men that Bill Bright would influence was Dave Hannah, who played football at Oklahoma State and then for the LA Rams but was injured and had to discontinue his career. He developed a campus ministry with college athletes called Athletes in Action.

At first Bright took his stand with the fundamentalists. In fact he arranged with Bob Jones University that he would continue to recruit BJU graduates as long as they would send students to Campus Crusade. He assured BJU that he would stand shoulder-to-shoulder with BJU against all forms of compromise, including the ecumenical evangelism of Billy Graham. Sadly, he succumbed to compromise at Graham's San Francisco Crusade at Cow Palace: ten BJU graduates quit on the spot. Campus Crusade was built with weak board members who were not separatists, men such as Daniel Fuller, Dr. Harold Ockenga, and liberal Mark Hatfield.

Dr. Charles Dunn, former faculty advisor for Campus Crusade at Clemson University, summarizes best the weaknesses of Campus

Crusade in his booklet *Campus Crusade: Its Message and Methods.* In this booklet he says,

> "The secular college and university campuses are vast spiritual deserts that need the refreshment of the biblical oasis. All too many organizations and churches have become mirages on these spiritual deserts. Campus Crusade, once an oasis, has increasingly become a mirage. The campus needs the message of regeneration and reformation, not of compromise and cultural accommodation."[10]

Dunn states that "the umbrella of the New Evangelical movement is so broad as to contain Roman Catholics, Charismatics and members of denominations that hold to Modernist and Neo-orthodox views. They overlook that apostasy is like cancer."[11] Again he warns that "the Campus Crusade message that they are taught by design or default includes not using 'Christian jargon' like: witness, repent, converted, blood, hell, sin, save, holiness and apostasy."[12] The reason: these are not "soft" or "cool" words. 2 Timothy 1:13 commands believers "to hold fast the form of sound words." There is no doubt that the theology of Campus Crusade substitutes the world's terminology for God's terminology. The slogan "I found it" originated with Campus Crusade, reducing Christ to "it." Campus Crusade for Christ has made prolific use of their little booklet "The Four Spiritual Laws."

Baptism is not taught or followed, yet Campus Crusade boasts of how it is fulfilling the Great Commission. Their outreach method is to follow the "Big Domino" Theory, to reach first the influential people on campus: the athletes and the sorority and fraternity leaders. Like each of the parachurch organizations, they like to put the imprimatur of their organization on the local church. A Crusade staff worker said, "Campus Crusade is not a church, so we are not responsible for all of Scripture."[13] Often they will infiltrate

---

[10]Charles Dunn, *Campus Crusade: Its Message and Methods* (Greenville: Bob Jones University Press, 1982), 2.

[11]Ibid., 8.

[12]Ibid., 9.

[13]George Dollar, "Critique of the Four Spiritual Laws of Campus Crusade," *Faith for the Family*, May/June 1975, 22.

liberal churches and will appear to be spiritual giants in such dead churches. They lack accountability to anyone but themselves. Such parachurch groups are religion gone free enterprise.

The strengths of Campus Crusade have been Bill Bright's vision, burden, and organizational wizardry illustrated by the fact that Campus Crusade is the largest new evangelical organization in the world. In fifty years Bill Bright has built an organization that is based on a $45-million, 285-acre site and employs over 20,514 full-time staff workers and over 663,000 volunteers in 68 ministries in 181 countries.[14] In 1996 Bright won the $1.1 million Templeton Prize, which he promptly donated to his Fasting and Prayer ministry. His vision for ministry is seen in his recent New Life 2000 Campaign, where Campus Crusade asked people from all major denominations to join its full-time staff members in reaching 5000 million-population target areas and to plant 1 million new churches. "Many different denominations and missions agencies are answering Christ's call to unite and get the good news out quickly,"[15] says Dr. Ted Engstrom, president emeritus of World Vision. An advertisement invites people to "Join with other Christian leaders from all major denominations, para-church and lay ministries, pastors, businesses, the academic community, and the legal world. We invite your input and participation as we link arms to help fulfill the great commission."[16] Campus Crusade's motto has been, "Win the Campus to Christ today, win the world to Christ tomorrow." Campus Crusade has been known for its zeal in seeking to fulfill its mission statement. Bill Bright's emphasis on prayer in the early years of his ministry, which he has maintained throughout, is a convicting pattern for any ministry. Each fall, Campus Crusade distributes, at no cost to the student, 400,000 Freshman Survival Kits. Each kit contains a New Testament, Josh McDowell's book *More Than a Carpenter*, a music CD, an "issues" video, information on how to become a Christian, and directions on how to log on to a web site that answers questions about Christianity.

---

[14]The Ivy Jungle Network, "The Campus Ministry Update," November 2000.
[15] Ted Engstrom, advertising flyer, "New Life 2000," mailed in 1999.
[16]Ibid.

Lessons to Be Learned from the Leaders in New Evangelical Campus Ministries[17]

Campus Ministry	Positive Lessons	Negative Lessons
1. InterVarsity (The Academic Model)	1. Emphasizes the head (intellect) 2. Apologetics 3. Students doing the work of the ministry	1. Lack of accountability to the local church 2. Lack of obedience to the doctrine of separation 3. Poor campus leadership
2. Navigators (The Military Model)	1. Emphasizes the will (doing) 2. Discipleship materials, memory program 3. The marines of campus ministry in the past	1. Lack of accountability to the local church 2. Lack of obedience to the doctrine of separation
3. Campus Crusade (The Social Model) Athletes in Action and Fellowship of Christian Athletes (The Athletic Model)	1. Emphasizes the heart—emotion (zeal) 2. Highly organized ministry 3. Very good training program 4. Emphasis on prayer	1. Lack of accountability to the local church 2. Lack of obedience to the doctrine of separation

The lessons learned should be implemented in the fundamentalist's philosophy of campus ministry. The goal for the local church is to have an outreach to the college campus to fulfill the Great Commission. The campus ministry should strive to be balanced, ministering to the head, heart, and will of the student. Incorporated in the campus ministry should be a strong discipleship program using solid, biblically based materials. An emphasis on memory work should be incorporated in the diet of the student. The ministry

---

[17]Lecture notes of Dr. Charles Dunn on campus models at the annual Spurgeon Foundation Campus Ministries Conference, June 14, 1995, University Baptist Church, Clemson, SC.

should be well organized and geared to involve the student in doing the "work of the ministry"[18] while being properly overseen by competent spiritual leaders. Campus workers should be well trained and able to disciple others.

The two necessary hallmarks setting the fundamentalist campus ministry apart from new evangelical ones should be sound doctrine and a strong relationship to the local church. There should also be a long-term vision, burden, and model for establishing multiple campus ministries within the state, nation, and world, which would involve a training base for campus workers. At the local level the church needs to have a clear picture as to its best organizational model for reaching the students, plus an awareness of the successful elements found in parachurch ministry models and of the need to maintain doctrinal purity. With this in place the church is ready to start the chartering process to enter the campus.

---

[18]Eph. 4:12.

5

STARTING A CAMPUS MINISTRY

A campus ministry could be started informally with several college students and could accomplish a great deal for the Lord, as seen by what one student who was saved at college wrote in his journal:

> In addition to the Saturday evening meeting, I fed my faith at a meeting every Sunday evening with six other believing students. Before I left the university, the number increased to twenty. In these meetings, one or more of the brethren prayed, we read Scriptures, sang hymns, someone exhorted the group, and we read some edifying writings of godly men. I opened my heart to the brethren for prayer and encouragement to keep me from backsliding.[1]

This informal campus ministry had many of the key elements to making a successful campus ministry, but not all student organizations are led by students like George Muller. Regarding such a campus ministry, Muller stated that the

> Lord and the Word were so exciting to me that I could not wait until Saturday came again. Now my life became very different, although I did not give up every sin at once. I did give up my wicked companions, going to taverns, and habitual lying. I read the Scriptures, prayed often, loved the brethren, went to church with the right motives, and openly professed Christ although my fellow students laughed at me.[2]

---

[1]George Muller, *The Autobiography of George Muller* (Springdale, Pa.: Whitaker House, 1984), 20.

[2]Ibid., 17.

What Muller describes happening to him at college is what fundamentalists should desire for every college student. The campus ministry should be exciting, and meetings where the "Lord and the Word" is the source and the object of one's excitement should be longed for. This is obviously a supernatural work. People can plan, organize, and do everything right, but unless the Lord builds the campus ministry, they labor in vain. Muller's experience is an excellent example of a student saved at college who at first found most of his fellowship and teaching with a group of believers on campus. Later, Muller would find his way to the local church, but sadly there were no Bible-preaching churches in his college town. He writes, "Although I regularly went to church when I did not preach myself, I seldom heard the truth because there was no enlightened clergyman in the town. When Dr. Tholuck or any other godly minister preached, I often walked ten or fifteen miles to enjoy the privilege of hearing the Word."[3] His story illustrates the need of having a Bible-believing church in a college town and a campus ministry with strong campus presence.

PREPARING THE CHURCH FOR THE CAMPUS MINISTRY

It is imperative for the local church to recognize the need of an on-campus presence to have an effective outreach to college students. The campus is where the students are. The campus, then, is the fishing hole where the fisher of men must take his tackle box. Occasionally, college students may stumble into churches on Sunday. But that is rare, and without immediate and careful follow-up, they will not generally return. In addition, it takes time for some students to darken the doors of a church. Dr. Darren Dawson, an engineering professor at Clemson, states that "the church is very intimidating to many non-Christians, especially foreign students."[4]

Also, churches need to understand that many college students go home on weekends. Many colleges are known as "suitcase" colleges,

---

[3] Ibid., 20.
[4] Darren Dawson, interview by William J. Senn III, January 29, 1999.

where the majority of the students head home on Thursday or Friday and do not return until Sunday night or Monday morning. Who can blame them for running home to mama's cooking after eating at the college cafeteria during the week? Therefore, the campus ministry must be a seven-day-a-week ministry, and much attention must be given to winning and training students during the week. This does not mean that the local church does not maximize its services on Sunday; it simply means that some students won't be reached unless the church ministers on the campus during the week. Also, this means that the campus ministry may minister to students that the local church will never see. Some churches are not readily accessible to the campus. Obviously, the closer the church is to the campus the better, but churches up to fifteen miles or even a half-hour drive away can still have an effective ministry.

To start a campus ministry, the pastor of the local church must have a burden and a vision for such a work. If the pastor is not behind this ministry, the campus ministry will flounder in the ocean of discouragement. The pastor must then bring his pastoral staff and deacons on board with his goal to start a campus ministry and instruct them as to which organizational model he believes is best in reaching the campus from their church. The pastor then needs to prepare his flock for such ministry. It is extremely important for the local church to realize that the college in their backyard is not merely an option for evangelizing but that they are commanded to "go"[5] into all the world and preach the gospel. They must accept the fact that God has providentially and in His sovereignty placed their church in arm's reach of the college campus with the clear intention for them to give out the gospel. The pastor needs to be prepared to receive some negative feedback about reaching the town's campus. Sadly, many churches do not see their responsibility to include the campus ministry in their scope of outreaches. This heartless shortsightedness has hindered many a campus ministry. There are potentially many reasons that the church family will resist a campus ministry, such as the following:

[5]Mark 16:15.

75

REASONS LOCAL CHURCHES DO NOT HAVE A CAMPUS MINISTRY

1. Intimidated by the intellectualism of the campus.

2. Selfishly asking what the church gains from college students who cannot tithe much or give much.

3. Justifying their overlooking of campus ministry because the students are not locals who will stay in the area but are very transient.

4. Fearing the negative influences of worldly and ungodly students on their own youth.

5. Ignorance: not knowing how to minister to college students.

6. Anti-education, ignorant ones who ridicule the educated.

7. The fear of being overrun by college students.

8. Laziness: not wanting to add any more work or projects to the church ministries list.

9. Stinginess: not wanting to spend any money for such a ministry.

10. Shortsightedness in seeing the potential of reaching college students.

11. Impatience: not willing to give campus ministry time and having unrealistic expectations.

12. Blindness to the mission field: "You can't build a church on college students."

CHARTERING THE CAMPUS MINISTRY

To have the most effective campus ministry, the church needs to charter a student organization. Once chartered, the ministry will have an official campus presence and will be able to meet on the campus, use classrooms and lecture halls, advertise, use the campus postal system for mass mail-outs, distribute literature, gain access to student lists (e.g., international students, students who are Baptists), conduct outdoor evangelistic services, and conduct a full-scale campus ministry.

To secure a charter, the church should find out from the college how to charter a student organization. This information is usually found in the student handbook of the university. Typically the following requirements are needed to be a recognized student organization: a petition signed by students currently enrolled at the university (the number of signatures varies from school to school), a faculty advisor, a constitution and by-laws, and a list of student officers. Some colleges do not require this much detail; instead, they may have the student inquiring fill out an application for establishing a campus organization, or they may simply verbalize their permission to proceed.

Petition

Often the university will ask for a petition signed by current students that shows interest in establishing a student campus organization. The number of signatures will vary. Because the petition simply demonstrates that there is student interest for such an organization, the students on the list do not have to be members of the local church; however, it would be best to first gather the names of those who attend the sponsoring church or other fundamental churches in town or in the state. If more signatures are needed on the petition form, the church can commission students in the church to present the vision and need to fellow students. Getting a petition signed will not be a problem; getting faithful members might be.

Faculty Advisor

A more difficult task may be finding the faculty advisor for the group. The pastor or campus worker should first survey his own congregation; if there is a faculty member or employee of the local college, ask him to be the liaison between the students and the university. From the school's viewpoint, the faculty advisor is just an advisor and a contact person. The university will mail all or most organizational literature to the faculty advisor and/or the student officers. If any problems with the student organization surface, the university will communicate with the advisor. From the viewpoint of the university, he is an organizational oversight component; from the local church's viewpoint, he is that and ideally a spiritual advisor. The campus advisor should attend some of the campus ministry's activities and meetings during the year. The more the faculty advisor can be involved, the stronger the campus ministry will become.

If the local church does not have a qualified employee of the university, the church can inquire at other fundamental churches in the area to see if someone from their congregations would volunteer to fill the gap for the campus organization. If the local church cannot find a faculty advisor, they will need to pray one in and, if need be, go win one to the Lord. Because the majority of the leadership and direction for the campus ministry is coming from the pastor and his campus worker delegate, the advisor could be a young convert.

Constitution and By-Laws

Generally the university will give the group a sample constitution and by-laws for them to follow. The constitution needs to be very simple, generic, and truthful. It should have the minimum information needed and no more. Some colleges will require that the group sign a statement that it will not discriminate on the basis of race, religion, or sexual orientation. This is a difficult document to dance around. The church should fill out the form as far as conscience permits and make it emphatically clear that the organization is open for any university students to attend. Most universities recognize that a religious organization would desire that its officers and leadership be of the same persuasion as defined by the mission statement of the organization. For the Christian group, they recognize that the group would not desire for a Muslim to be the group's president. The stickier issue comes when a lesbian wants to be the group's secretary. At the present time most universities are willing to work with these exceptions.

Student Officers

Most university forms require each organization to cite its student officers. The first year, these officers should be appointed by the pastor and/or campus worker and should be the most faithful students or contacts the local church has. Again, the leadership for the campus ministry will be generated primarily by the leadership of the local church; therefore, the officers, like the faculty advisor, can be young converts.

As the campus ministry develops over the years, the officers will play a larger role in the implementation of the mission statement.

For example, when first establishing a campus ministry, the campus pastor may have to do much of the planning for activities. However, as the ministry develops, he will work with the student officers to solicit input from the students as to their fellowship and activity interests and coordinate a game plan. The student officers will then do most of the implementing of the plan. The sooner the campus worker can delegate this aspect of the campus ministry, the better.

Typically, the campus ministry will have a president, vice president, treasurer, and secretary; other officers and committees can be added formally or informally. Such leadership will be needed to handle various aspects: the campus ministry's website; the campus news-letter, which should be produced at the beginning or end of each semester; advertising needs; designs for shirts, sweatshirts, caps, or other items; and other needs that arise. The president will generally serve as one of the platform workers for the weekly campus meeting and needs to be faithful to all the meetings. He will assist the campus worker in the delegation of the master plan for campus ministries. The vice president will assist the president and the campus worker in organizing and delegating the various aspects of the campus calendar. The treasurer will keep records of the finances and will handle the necessary monies. He will need to keep good records when handling monies for the various activities, trips, sports outreach tournaments, and other events. The secretary keeps track of the attendance records and the membership of the group. He is to take notes for each of the meetings and chronicle the events of the school year.

Approval Process and Future Requirements

After all the necessary information is compiled, it is submitted to the university for approval. The approval process may take several weeks or several months; the church should plan accordingly and, if need be, ask for interim approval to start meeting on campus. Most colleges are encouraged to see students wanting to form organizations; this looks good both in their student handbook and on the student's resume.

Each year the organization will need to fill out an updated form listing that year's officers and any changes to the constitution and by-laws. Also, each year the organization will be asked to have its picture taken for the student organization section of the school's yearbook.

Once approved, the church will have a wide-open door to minister to students on the campus. Before beginning the ministry the campus worker should read the university's student handbook for any rules that may pertain to religious activities on campus. Some colleges will not allow people to go door-to-door in the dormitories, making "cold calls" with students. Violating university regulations may cause the organization to lose its charter or cause other problems. For example, Baptist Mid-Missions missionary Steve Giegerich received a letter from the assistant vice president of residence life at Notre Dame, where his campus ministry was chartered:

> I am requesting that you no longer enter upon any University property or enter a University residence facility to speak with students or distribute materials on behalf of Campus Bible Fellowship or any other organization. Should you continue to engage in the activities not permitted by University policies, procedures or regulations, I will be required to issue you a trespass letter. The issuance of such a letter would result in your arrest for criminal trespass if violated.[6]

Obviously, most campuses will not be as hard-nosed as Notre Dame University when it comes to distributing Christian literature, but it is important that workers know what is permitted and what is not. There are so many ways to get the gospel out on the college campus that the group does not want to jeopardize its charter foolishly. It is imperative that the campus worker instruct any interns, extension workers, and campus helpers of the parameters for campus ministry as drawn by the university.

Once the campus ministry is approved to minister on the secular campus, to whom does it minister? How does it find and reach the George Mullers?

---

[6]William W. Kirk, letter to Steve Giegerich, September 13, 1999.

6

The Fivefold Scope of Campus Ministry

Today there are over 15 million students enrolled in American colleges, universities, and institutes. However, the scope of campus ministry is even larger than that. A common oversight for churches is to miss the full extent of what truly is campus ministry. Campus ministry can be divided into five areas: undergraduate students, graduate students, young married couples, international students, and faculty and staff. Each group represented has similar needs as well as unique needs. The campus worker should be aware of these needs and plan his ministry accordingly to meet the needs of each group.

The spiritual needs of those within the scope of the campus ministry are no different from those of any other sinner on the earth. They need to call on the Lord as their personal Savior. They need to be surrendered to the will of God. They need to be holy and seek to be more like Christ each day, and they need to be involved in the Lord's work. These goals are the same for each of the areas of campus ministry. The message never changes, but the method in communicating these goals may take on a little different approach for each group.

The Undergraduate Students

In most colleges undergraduate students make up the largest percentage of the student body. Consequently the ministry to the undergraduate should be given significant emphasis. This is the group that people typically think of when they think of campus ministry. It is also the group that is targeted by the other organizations. These groups are very competitive in recruiting undergraduates and will seek to sway the undergraduates to be a part of their ministry, in many cases from the very first day of the school year. Some campus organizations even start recruiting freshmen by manning booths during the orientation days for the freshmen and their families.

It is an observable pattern to see "Joe Freshman" come to college from a Christian home, and if he does not get quickly involved in a good church or campus ministry, by the time he graduates, he will have little to no interest in spiritual things. Christians who do not get attached to a church or campus ministry will usually end up as shipwrecks of the faith.

Undergraduate students seem to have the most free time on their hands. They enjoy many different activities all of the time. They are full of energy and excitement and need to be challenged regularly. If the campus ministry does not plan enough activities, the undergraduates will find something else to do or some other group to do it with. They frequently jump from group to group and regularly are seen involved in several campus ministries. They enjoy being with fellow undergraduates, typically those within a year or two of their own age and academic status. Their friends are typically those from back home, their dormitory, their classes, and their social and sports interests.

On the state campus there is a great push to join a fraternity or a sorority, and in many cases the campus worker will encounter students in these "Animal Houses." These are no place for the Christian, and believers should be urged to remove themselves from their ranks. They are a great place to minister to, but Christians should not want to live there.

The undergraduate student is undergoing many transitions and has many needs that can be addressed in Sunday school and/or in the campus meetings. The Sunday school class should be geared just for undergraduate students, and activities and fellowships should be reinforced through the Sunday school class.

Undergraduate students need to be made to feel comfortable in the campus ministry and the church. Therefore, for the most part, keep the undergraduate students separated from the graduate students. Graduate students typically come across as intellectual and spiritual superiors and arrogant in their accrued knowledge, which is a real "turn-off" to undergraduates. Undergraduates want their own ministry!

In addition, the "church kids" who have gone to Christian schools all their lives need to be welcoming towards the visiting secular college students and make them feel at home. In addition, undergraduate students thrive on families in the church taking an interest in them and providing meals and a refreshing family atmosphere.

The undergraduate ministry can become a real soap opera with many dating heartbreaks and issues. This will be one area in which the campus worker will especially need to give biblical instruction.

Today's undergraduate is looking to have a fun time at college. The wise campus worker will meet him at that level and take him to higher ground.

Key Ministry Areas Within the Church for Undergraduate Students

1. Undergraduate student ministries (Just as David served his "own generation,"[1] the undergraduate can best reach his peers.)
2. Children's ministries
3. Youth ministries
4. Nursing home ministries
5. Sports outreaches

THE GRADUATE STUDENTS

Graduate students are a breed all their own. They are graduate students and will let anyone know it. People can ask them what they are studying, but they should not ask when they will finish! The beauty of ministering to graduate students, especially the PhD candidates, is that they become fixtures in the church. They become like in-laws

---

[1] Acts 13:36.

who never go home. All kidding aside, graduate students are a fruitful group to which to minister. Typically a graduate is a much more dedicated and serious student than the normal undergraduate. They rarely are found living in the dorms at this point in their academic careers and may have actually learned how to cook for themselves. They drive beat-up cars and work off hard drives. They are busy doing research, doing the dirty work of professors in "research," and at times teaching "Freshman Calculus 101."

This group needs fellowship but not as often as the undergraduate student. They enjoy Bible studies and the "meat" of the Word. Generally, graduate students want substantial and airtight answers to their theological questions. They see through interpretive inconsistencies and can argue either direction as to whether Adam and Eve had bellybuttons. They are a challenging group, which is why it is wise for a campus worker to have an undergraduate and graduate degree. By having both degrees, the campus worker will be a more credible witness to them.

Although there are some graduate students who can cross over and work with the undergraduate ministry, it is best to have a separate Sunday school class for the graduate students. However, there will be outreaches and activities, which will be discussed in chapter ten, where all aspects of the campus ministry will work together.

Graduate students can be effective workers in various ministries. If they are trained well, they will assume teaching roles with many of the younger classes in the church and will do a great job. Perhaps the most effective outreach ministry for the saved graduate student is with the international students. Most graduate students have natural and regular contacts with international students and are able to relate to them academically. Such contacts can easily lead into outreach opportunities with these students.

Key Ministry Areas Within the Church for Graduate Students
1. Graduate student ministries
2. One-on-one Bible studies with undergraduate students
3. International ministries
4. Children's ministries

5. Youth ministries

6. Nursing home ministries

7. Sports outreaches

THE YOUNG MARRIED COUPLES

Young married couples are a unique dimension of campus ministry. University towns are filled with married and unmarried couples living together, with one or both working on a degree at the university. Young couples who are still in school are easy to discern when they visit the church. While the undergraduate pulls up in a brand new Ford Mustang or Honda Accord and the graduate student drives in with a Volvo or Saab, the young married couple diesels in with a station wagon or a mini-van with paint chipping off of the hood. The wife usually is toting in a crying baby with a snotty nose, while the husband tries to tuck in his shirt and adjust his tie. This couple spells needs. They are living off of love and an assistantship and are facing ten years to pay off school bills and credit card debts. The husband keeps promising his wife that things will get better once he graduates, whenever that may be. She is lonely and wondering if it is worth it all. The baby simply does what she would like to do—cry. They need encouragement, exercise, and teaching on such topics as child-rearing, finances, and priorities. How refreshing it is for them to find a church that has an interest in married college students.

Another ministry need is ministering to couples that are not married but who are living together. A church with a campus ministry must expect to have such visitors who need the gospel and who will need to be confronted in due time regarding their housing arrangement.

Having a separate Sunday school class for this group is essential. Providing a nursery and some babysitting for the children would be heavenly for the mother, who lives in a duplex in the married housing section of the university without car or husband for most of the day and night and whose fellowship is having the baby wave at the garbage man on Monday mornings and listening to Abdul Bubba Wang cook the cat next door. What would a couples' retreat do for her? Young married couples who are attending college do not need the campus rallying point as much as the undergraduates do.

They feel much more comfortable attending church or home Bible studies.

Key Ministry Areas Within the Church for Young Married Couples

1. Evangelistic Bible studies with other young couples

2. International ministries

3. Undergraduate student ministries

4. Youth ministries

5. Children's ministries

6. Nursing home ministries

THE INTERNATIONAL STUDENTS

Perhaps the most exciting aspect of campus ministry is ministering to the international student. Today there are over 600,000 international students studying in America's colleges. Think about the potential as the cream of the crop, the future leaders of the world, come to Americans' backyards to study. The most remarkable fact is that the largest percentages of the international students come from the three most difficult parts of the world for the church to evangelize: China, India, and Muslim nations. Americans cannot easily go into any of these areas and plant churches and train nationals. However, God has brought them to America for Christians to reach and to train and to send back to reach their own people.

The campus worker should emphasize the international aspect of campus ministry when presenting the campus ministry to other churches. In my estimation, reaching international students while they are in the United States is the most cost-effective way of reaching the world. These students are highly educated, highly motivated people who are away from their families and friends and are wide open to learning English, American culture, and what has made America great: Bible Christianity. Once converted, baptized, and trained, these evangelists and missionaries return to their people knowing the language, knowing the culture, having the contacts, manifesting a changed life, and not needing a furlough. They can immediately get to work for the Lord. Most likely it was the international community meeting at the Hall of Tyrannus that made Paul's ministry so effective in getting the gospel to all of Asia Minor. I can see the students studying abroad at the Hall of Tyrannus, hearing the gospel preached and taught by Paul. Over a two-year period, they were trained to go back to other parts of Asia Minor to be "tentmakers" like Paul and preach the gospel.

In the Old Testament, God impressed upon His people the importance of ministering to the "stranger" (international student) in the land. In the same way, Christians should seek to minister to the international students in their communities. Because of the importance of this area of campus ministry, this dissertation devotes an entire chapter to ministering to international students.

Key Ministry Areas Within the Church for International Students
1. Evangelizing and training their fellow international students
2. Children's ministries
3. Youth ministries

FACULTY AND STAFF OF THE UNIVERSITY

The faculty and staff of the university compose the group that may assist and finance most aspects of the campus ministry. Members of this group live in the community and are employed by the university. Depending upon the size of the university, there may be hundreds or thousands of employees; they need the Lord too!

This group can ultimately represent part of the core or base that is needed in the local church to have an effective campus ministry. These people can provide stability for the campus ministry. They understand the needs of the college students as well as anyone and can assist in any adopt-a-student program that is developed. They are on the campus five days a week and can provide a respite for the student who just needs to talk with someone or get some advice. In addition, the Christian testimony of a faculty or staff member will be a great encouragement in the faith to students. The godly Christian professor will have, in many cases, a greater spiritual impact on the student than the pastor in the pulpit will.

One of the most effective ways of reaching faculty and staff members with the gospel is to have Bible studies on the campus just for them. The best time for such studies might be during the lunch hour. The Christian faculty and staff are strengthened by the fellowship and Bible study, and it also gives them a vehicle for inviting their colleagues that need to hear the gospel. These studies need to be precise and well presented. Most professors are highly trained in one specific area of study but have very little knowledge of the Bible. A book study (e.g., Genesis, Revelation) or a subject study (e.g., Creation, interpersonal relationships) on topics of interest can be effective in reaching the faculty, who especially need to hear the good news.

Key Ministry Areas Within the Church for Faculty and Staff
1. Acting as campus parents to students
2. Bible studies with fellow faculty members
3. Bible studies with staff and/or research assistants
4. International ministries
5. Young couple ministries
6. Graduate student ministries
7. Undergraduate student ministries
8. Youth ministries
9. Children's ministries
10. Nursing home ministries

Evaluating the key areas in which each group can minister proves that the faculty and staff of the college can become the local church's greatest asset in a full-fledged campus ministry. Special effort should be given to win them to the Lord and to train them to minister.

LADIES' MINISTRIES

Each aspect of the campus ministry can be subdivided further in order to focus attention on particular needs of the ladies' ministry. Because the campus worker is a man, it is not wise for him to enter the women's dormitory to conduct Bible studies and other ministries. Therefore, some of the mature women in the church or the campus ministry need to be trained to conduct soulwinning Bible studies and one-on-one discipleship training. Also, women are especially needed in ministering to the international wives and students. In some cultures, a man cannot have a ministry in any capacity with a married woman. It will be of the utmost importance to have some ladies equipped to reach out to internationals.

With women composing sixty percent of college students in America today, it would be advisable, in larger campus ministries or towns, to engage the services of a full-time ladies' worker. The pastor's wife and the campus worker's wife should play some part in the campus ministry, but their roles will be limited, especially if they have children, and time spent on campus will be minimal. To have an effective campus ministry, there must be constant campus presence, which a full-time ladies' worker can provide. Chapter thirteen will deal more thoroughly with the plea for campus missionaries and the need of lady campus missionaries to reach the college girls.

THE COMMUNITY COLLEGE STUDENT

The Campus Ministry Update states that in the fall of 2000, some 15.1 million students went to college in America.[2] Forty-four percent of those are attending one of America's 1,132 community colleges. The commuter student and the community college present a unique twist to campus ministry as the students are not living in dormitories on the campus. While many colleges are suitcase campuses on the weekend, the community college is a suitcase college seven days a week. The commuter student can still be reached while on campus through various outreach methods and is often very open to home Bible studies.

---

[2]The Ivy Jungle Network, "The Campus Ministry Update," October 10, 2000.

7

THE INTERNATIONAL MINISTRIES OF THE CAMPUS MINISTRY

The international student aspect of the college ministry is one of the most necessary. Today America has a very difficult time sending missionaries into the 10/40 window (latitudes) to reach China, India, and the more than twenty-eight Muslim nations, countries whose major religions are atheism, Islam, Hinduism, and Buddhism. This "window" is the least evangelized area in the world, yet the Lord has seen fit to send its future leaders to America.

CHINESE STUDENTS IN AMERICA

The largest portion of these students are coming from China. With over 1.3 billion citizens in China, the largest country in the world, each Chinese student in America represents approximately 50,000 people from the mainland of China. When someone says that these Chinese students are the cream of the crop, he is talking about the cream! Because China is closed to foreign missionaries but is open to sending its leaders to America for training, the best way for Americans to reach the Chinese is by reaching them in America on the college campuses.

In the late 1800s China was reluctantly open to foreign missionaries. The most famous of the English-speaking missionaries was Hudson Taylor. Taylor prayed in eighteen China Inland Mission (CIM) missionaries between 1876 and 1880. In 1885 the "Cambridge Seven" departed for China. In 1887, 100 more missionaries were accepted, many of them students from England and other countries who surrendered to the call of foreign missions. In 1900 the Boxer Rebellion resulted in the murder of fifty-eight CIM missionaries and twenty-one children. In 1905 China lost Hudson Taylor when he was taken home to be with the Lord. Fourteen years later, in 1919, the May 4th Student Movement took place, another setback for foreign missions. In 1926–27 nearly all 8,000 Protestant missionaries fled China during the chaos of the Northern Expedition, during which Chiang Kai-shek sought to unite China under the Kuomintang Party (KMT) and purge China of the Chinese Communist Party (CCP), which had been founded in 1921. In 1934 CIM missionaries John and Betty Stam were executed. During World War II most missionaries were either interned or evacuated from China. Those who remained or returned after the war were involved in the wholesale evacuation of China in 1951–52; the last CIM missionary left China on July 20, 1953. What a tragedy to trace the history of Protestant missionaries from 1807 to 1953![1]

Year	Number of Missionaries in China[2]
1807	1 (Englishman Robert Morrison, first Protestant missionary in Canton)
1840	20
1858	81
1865	189
1874	436
1893	1,324
1906	3,833
1918	6,395
1926	8,325
1928	4,375
1930	6,346
1953	0

[1]Austin, "Mission Dream Team," 19.
[2]Ibid., 41.

It is tragic that 100 years after Hudson Taylor went to China there would be literally no official foreign missionaries in China. Fortunately, God's great love for the Chinese did not cease in 1953. Through His providential work He has presented the English-speaking church with the opportunity to reach the Chinese through Chinese students as they attend American colleges.

How long will China continue to send her students to America? At present America is enjoying the fourth wave of students permitted to come to this country. The first wave of Chinese students took place in April of 1847, with the three Huang brothers coming to New York. They were the fruit of the Overseas Movement. In 1870 the Qing dynasty selected 120 boys, ages 12 to 15, to come to America and study in different groups. Then in 1881 all Chinese students were required to return to China. The second wave of Chinese students was in 1909, when the United States government assisted Chinese students in coming to America by funding overseas study. The monies were funded in part by the Chinese government's war reparations due to the Boxer Rebellion. This time the Qing dynasty sent one hundred students a year for the first four years and then sent fifty students a year. This practice continued even after the birth of the Republic of China in 1911. By this time there were over 1,000 mainland Chinese in America. This number increased to 3,900 by 1949. Some of the overseas students during this time were

1. Sun Yat-sen
2. Hu Shi
3. Zhou Enlai
4. Deng Xiaoping
5. Jiang Kaishe

How radically different China would be today if a campus ministry had been prepared to minister to that group when they arrived in the States! Such leaders, if they had trusted Christ, could have influenced over a billion Chinese for the Lord. Could the next Sun Yat-sen or Deng Xiaoping be sitting in one of America's campuses right now? Will Christians reach him with the gospel while he is in the States?

The third wave of students came to America between 1911 and 1949. During this period China experienced the May 4, 1919

Student Movement; the birth of the Chinese Communist party; the Northern Expedition; and the Sino-Japanese War (1937–1945), during which China lost Taiwan to Japan and lost Korea to independence. Despite all these events, by 1949 there were 3,900 Chinese students studying in America.

When the Communists took control of China in 1949, they closed the door to students coming to America. From 1949 to 1978 China followed the closed-door policy of Russia. Also during this period China experienced the Cultural Revolution (1966–1976) and the Anti-Gang-of-Four-Rally on Tiananmen Square in 1976. Following Mao's death in 1976, Chairman Deng Xiaoping opened the door in 1978 for the fourth wave of students to come to America. Hopefully, this time the door will never be shut, and Lord willing, China will open its door to foreign missions.

Chairman Mao wrote a book called *The Works of Mao Zedong* in which he lists Christianity as a "religion, superstition, and reactionary cult."[3] The Chinese were taught pure atheism, and if they were to worship any god, it would be Mao Zedong; if they were to revere any book, it would be the little "Red Book of Chairman Mao." This impacts the recent history of ministry to Chinese students. They generally come to America with little to no knowledge of Christianity or the Bible. How sad to see the descendants of Shem who once worshiped the true God turn their eyes from God to man!

THE PRECIOUSNESS OF LIFE

attributed to Emperor K'ang Hsi (1662–1723), Ching Dynasty
The precious things of heaven are: sun, moon, and stars.
The precious things of earth are: five grains, gold and silver.
A nation's essential precious things are upright faithful statesmen.
A family's essential precious things are filial sons and virtuous grandsons.

---

[3]Ambassadors for Christ, *Mainland Chinese in America: An Emerging Kinship* (Paradise, PA: Ambassadors for Christ, 1991), 44.

Gold and White gems are not really precious; only 'eternal'
life is always great!
One hundred years is thirty-six thousand days;
But if one does not have life, then surely most pitiful.
When one comes and is foolish; then when he leaves he
will perish!
Even if one should eat all the delightfully flavored food,
And his body be clothed with the royal apparel of the
king's court,
Even tho' traveling on all the five lakes and four seas in
deluxe accommodations,
How would that place him in the Emperor's family?
The greatest thing on earth is the matter of life and death!
White gems and gold are useless!
Even poor food and clear rice gruel can satisfy hunger.
Even if you had elegant clothing, could you wear them
several thousand years?
Heaven's gate was long ago closed to our first ancestors.
But the road to bliss has been opened the whole way.
By the work of the Holy Son, and by Him alone!
I desire to receive this Holy Son of God,
And with the status of sonship, obtaining eternal life.[4]

During the last fifty years the Chinese government has not had
"upright faithful statesmen" but ungodly men who have sought to
eliminate philosophies, cultures, political and economic theories, and
anything that opposed Communism. Most Chinese students now
in America were born during or after the Cultural Revolution. Their
parents and grandparents suffered terribly during this time, leaving a
bitter mark against Communism for them. Fueling this bitterness and
the student's distrust of Communism further was the student protests
in Tiananmen Square in April and May of 1989, culminating on June
4 with government tanks deliberately running over the protesters.

During the fourth wave of Chinese students, which continues
today, approximately one out of every two international students is
Chinese. They are spread throughout America: 29.8 percent in the
Northeast, 26.6 percent in the Midwest, 15.4 percent in the South,

---

[4]Fred Nelson, trans., "Preciousness of Life."

15.2 percent in the West Coast, 8.4 percent in the Southwest, and 4.4 percent in the Mountain region.[5] Eighty percent of the Chinese students are men. Ninety-five percent of the Chinese come with no knowledge of any religion. One Chinese professor summed it up best: "We do not believe in God; we do not believe in the Communist Party; we do not believe in anything."[6] In many ways the hearts of the Chinese students are blank slates for Christians to write indelibly upon the message of the true "son of heaven." In the 1990s China more frequently began allowing the male student's wife, and sometimes his children and parents, to come to the States as well. International ministries now include ministering to potentially three generations. For example, on Easter 2001, University Baptist Church baptized a grandmother, her daughter, and her granddaughter, all of whom had trusted Christ as their Savior since coming to the States.

The Chinese students are being emphasized in this study to illustrate the abounding opportunities to minister to international students. The Chinese also represent a large percentage of the international student body. For example, in 2000, Berkeley University alone had an incoming freshman class of which forty-five percent were of Asian descent, thirty percent white, nine percent Hispanic, and only four percent African-American.[7] However, the international ministry should target all the international students.

MINISTERING TO INTERNATIONAL STUDENTS

The best way to minister to the international students is to know their spiritual, academic, social, and physical needs. After an international student attains either an F-1 Visa (which is a student visa and usually privately sponsored) or a J-1 Visa (which is for the advanced student or scholar who is officially funded by the student's country), he is ready to take off for America. (The F-2 or J-2 Visas are for the family members of either the F-1 or J-1 student.) In many cases this is their first flight anywhere. For those coming from the

---

[5]The Ivy Jungle Network, "The Campus Ministry Update," November 2000.
[6]Chinese professor, interviewed by Gary Balius, December 1996.
[7]The Ivy Jungle Network, "The Campus Ministry Update," November 2000.

Orient or from India, the trip to America will take around twenty-four hours. Imagine your first flight on Dragon Air to Hong Kong and then your connecting flight to Detroit, where you need to find your next flight and are given directions to the area by a true New Yorker. You are all alone; all of your earthly belongings have been squeezed into two suitcases and a carry-on; and you are unsaved. You finally arrive at the Atlanta airport, where you are to meet a "Bubba," whom you have never met before and who is to take you to your dormitory room, which is sandwiched between two rooms that smell of marijuana and stale beer.

This scenario can be improved by the Christian, who can minister to international students by meeting them at the airport and taking them to their housing arrangement. The university will be glad to have someone assist them in these arrangements and can provide such contacts and flight information. Make arrangements for a follow-up visit to assist the student in getting oriented to his new location. A nice touch would be to have a small welcome basket waiting for him. The international student will be a friend for life if the Christian demonstrates just a little thoughtfulness.

International Dinners and Flea Market

At the beginning of the fall semester the local church should host an international dinner/day and flea market. This event can be promoted by mail-outs, e-mails, phone calls, and by word of mouth. Often the university can make available the university's list of international students enrolled.

At this event, which can be an all-day event or simply an evening, the church will want to provide a meal. It will be important to have foods for vegetarians on the menu. The evening should include a special program acknowledging all of the guests and the various countries they represent. Special music, testimonies, and a gospel presentation are the key ingredients of the program. Students can wear native dress and, if desired, bring a food plate that would be typical from their country.

Visitor cards should be filled out when the students arrive at the church and receive their information packet on the church and its various international ministries. At the welcome center they should also receive some "funny" money to "purchase" items at the flea market. After the preaching, church members should hand out a question form asking if the student would like to have a personal Bible study. This form will be the key follow-up document. For those who mark "yes," a church member should make plans to have an evangelistic Bible study with them. (One such evangelistic study is *The Sower Series*, which will be introduced in the chapter on evangelism.) For most of the international students, this event will be the first time they have ever heard a gospel presentation. It typically takes weeks, months, and even years for many of the international students to be saved, but the workers should be patient; the seed is being sown at the international dinner, and there will be a harvest. The church needs to remember that some students are coming from an atheistic communistic system; others perceive Christianity as incompatible with being Chinese or incompatible with science. Other people will fear what others will think regarding their association with Christians or religion.

The church can meet some of the students' physical needs on this occasion through the "flea market," which is basically a glorified garage sale at which the students "purchase" kitchenware, furniture, clothes, bikes, and other items with the "funny" money given them when they arrived. The items for the flea market are donated by the church family, who have kept in mind throughout the year items from their garages, sheds, and attics that they no longer use or need and that they think the students could use. One person's junk is another's treasure. In addition, men in the church can bring their trucks and deliver newly "purchased" furniture for the students.

Over time, the international dinner can evolve into an international fair or carnival with activities such as a dunking booth, fire truck "tours," and games for the kids. The international dinner is a big hit with the students and will involve many people from the church and provide contacts that will take most of the first semester to follow up on.

International English Classes
On the heels of the international dinner, the church should begin international English classes. These classes can be offered during the day or at night and are designed for the wives of the international students and for struggling students who need extra assistance in English. A variety of classes can be offered, including an English Bible class, an American history class using a Christian textbook, a literature class using books such as *Pilgrim's Progress* with worksheets, an American culture and customs class, a TOEFL class to prepare those who need to take this English proficiency test, or a writing class.

Students will generally need rides, but pick-up locations around the international community of the college town are usually easy to find. The church will also need to provide a nursery, and the nursery workers need to be gladiators. Classes will last one hour with a break between classes, during which coffee and donuts are offered. The classes should meet once a week and follow the campus calendar for the fall and spring semesters (typically fourteen classes per semester). This outreach opportunity will bear tremendous fruit as the students learn of the Bible through each of the classes.

Additional related ministries could be to provide free editing services, which will encourage students writing papers to seek the church's help and will be deeply appreciated. And for the Christian international students, a Bible institute could be conducted on a weeknight during which students could be taught a Bible class or watch a video class (e.g., Dr. Jim Berg's counseling tapes) for actual credit or audit.

Driving Services
Offering a driving school, where church members teach international students to drive and then take them to the highway department to receive their permits and to take their driver's license tests, is another service that will be of great help to the student. This ministry is for the few and the brave, but it is an effective inroad with international students.

Another service related to this is to help the student select a used car. Many students have never purchased a car before and will not know what to look for. They will also not know how to maintain the car, so a maintenance class at the church could be offered.

Those students who cannot drive or cannot afford a car would benefit from a church member offering them his services as a "taxi" when needed. The students normally will not take advantage of such kindness offered and will be relieved to know that if they had to go to the store or to the hospital, they have someone who is available to help them.

International Sports Outreaches

Not all international students will need help with their English or their driving, so the church needs to develop ministries to appeal to their other interests. Most international students will be extremely intimidated in coming to church services, although they should still be invited to the service and a meal at an American home afterwards. However, the campus worker or others in the church will have a hard time at first getting some students, particularly the Muslims, to visit a church service to hear the gospel. But by using sports outreaches, the church can gather international students with the aim of presenting the gospel and inviting them to trust Christ.

Some of the international students enjoy sports. Most international students are very familiar with soccer (football), and those who play it are very good. Indian students go bananas over cricket and during the world cup can be found glued to satellite TV in the wee hours of the morning cheering their team on. The Chinese are extremely good at Ping-Pong. Most international students would love to learn how to play America's favorite pastime sport, baseball, in the form of softball. With these interests in mind, the local church with an international outreach can conduct various sports tournaments, such as a soccer tournament with almost an Olympic flavor as the various countries submit teams. The teams enjoy a well-organized tournament, a free meal, and the openly promoted Bible challenge. The Bible challenge should conclude with the visitors being asked if they would like further information on Christianity and if they would like a personal Bible study. This format will open up many follow-up opportunities for conversations on the Bible and salvation.

A reversal to the church organizing a tournament is to ask the Indian students to put on a cricket presentation and invite people to come and watch. After the demonstration the Indians can form teams, mixing in novice Americans. Such an arrangement can open up some real witnessing opportunities with the Indian students.

Arranging for an international softball league with proper instruction on how to play is another great way to meet students. They love to learn the game and, when someone actually catches a pop-up, will respond as if it were the last out of the World Series. After each game of the six-week season, a coach, player, or other church member should give a Bible challenge and an invitation to trust Christ.

The sports outreach concept is especially effective with the children of international students. The McDonald's approach to church is not so bad. If the kids want to come, the parents will often follow, especially to watch Yaki Saki Knok Yur Bloki play soccer with the American and international kids. International children should be also invited to participate in the church's Vacation Bible School, Awana-like programs, and other children's ministries. Often the parents or mothers will come for the entire program just to observe and learn themselves.

International Students and Holiday Participation
International students are intrigued with American culture and holidays. Every holiday provides a witnessing opportunity for the in-touch Christian. Easter and Christmas are natural times to present the gospel in an explanation of the significance of each holiday. Thanksgiving also lends itself nicely to explain why Christians are so thankful and Whom they thank.

International students delight in visiting American homes and sharing in holiday celebrations. They especially enjoy Christmas with all the lights and decorations. A Christmas light tour can be planned, and they can be invited to join any Christmas caroling programs. They will be amazed to hear Christians sing at nursing homes and to neighbors.

The Fourth of July presents an opportunity to promote patriotism, and if someone really wanted to turn some heads, he should take some students from mainland China and have them watch him vote. This activity will be very impressive to them as they watch freedom in action, assuming America can count the votes right. Weddings can provide another opportunity to present the gospel as most international students have never observed a Christian wedding in a church.

The Lord has given Americans so many object lessons with holidays and celebrations that Christians would be remiss not to include internationals in observing these occasions with them. This can be done informally, or it can be promoted with an adopt-an-international-student program for the holiday. But it does not take a holiday to have an international student come to someone's house. The international student has a great interest in just being in an American house with an American family. The American home greatly intrigues them and provides one of the Christian's greatest drawing cards.

In addition to celebrating holidays with an international student, Christians can really capitalize on building a friendship and presenting the gospel by expressing interest in their holidays. The Chinese New Year in many ways parallels the practices of the Jewish Passover in Exodus 12. They will stand in awe when they realize that the Jews would put blood around their doors much like they place their red paper around the sides and top of their doors. It is great fun to participate in the celebration of the Year of the Rat, Horse, Rabbit, etc. with them, and the Chinese food is delicious. The Chinese Fall Moon Festival, much like America's Thanksgiving, is another glorious occasion to congregate and to present the Creator's goodness.

International Retreats and Outings/Trips

One of the best opportunities to get to know international students is to include them on a trip, whether it be over the hill to grandmother's house at Christmas or during some other time of year to some other place. International students are typically very diligent in their studies as well as very frugal with their finances. However, they have great interest in seeing America. In many cases they have seen more of America than have the Americans. One should not be surprised to hear of their adventures to Disney World; Washington, D.C.; or New York City.

The best times for a campus ministry to plan official retreats and trips are during the shorter fall break, the longer spring break, or the summer months between summer school sessions. These retreats should be made affordable and should always tie in with a church service and/or daily Bible challenges. The purposes for the outing are for the student

- to see special segments of America
- to enjoy something historical, cultural, amusing, beautiful, etc. on the trip
- to hear the gospel
- to observe the testimonies of Christians over an extended period of time
- to give saved students an opportunity to invite unsaved students and families on the trip
- to strengthen the faith of the saved
- to further strengthen the ties to the local church ministry
- to further acquaint international students with the pastors and members of the church

The home church benefits because the trip will strengthen the relationships with the internationals and will allow greater integration to take place within the church's ministry. It will also increase the church's burden for the international outreach and missions, and most important, the trip will give church members the opportunity to give their testimony and witness.

When planning a trip with overnight stops, the campus worker or international worker should arrange for members of a sister church where the group will be visiting to host an international student or family. This arrangement brings the mission field right into their living room and will increase their burden for campus ministry and for reaching the world. It also cuts down considerably on the cost of the trip, which will always be a factor. Church gyms, prophet's chambers, and campgrounds could also be used for meeting the housing needs of the students.

If the local church has saved international students, everyone would receive a tremendous blessing from hearing their testimonies during a church service or, if so desired, from the international Christians conducting the entire service with special music, testimonies, and a message. To really maximize the visit, the host church could have a dinner on the grounds or a fellowship after the service. The more the host church can be involved with the students, the better. To tie this in with a missions conference is the icing on the cake. Imagine having students from all over the world at a missions conference! For many of the students, this visit will be only their second encounter with a true Christian church, and they will be very impressed with the network of churches.

Counseling Ministries

When dealing with people, there will be problems; and believe it or not, international students also have problems at times. Their problems will include academic problems, financial problems, housing problems, family problems, visa problems, and legal problems. Therefore, the active international ministry should have members who are competent to counsel.

The number one problem for international students will be domestic violence. These students face tremendous pressures. They are in a foreign country with a different culture and are being taught in a different language. The academic pressures alone are enormous. Adding to the frustration are generally the pressure of finances, the question of future employment, the absence of family and friends from back home, and exhaustion. Now add to this time bomb a wife who can hardly speak English; who has no car, no money, no mother; who stares at four walls all day, waiting for her preoccupied husband to come home for a few minutes to watch him stare at a computer screen. Needless to say, it does not take too much to trigger an explosion. Most international students are not aware of American laws as they relate to husbands abusing their wives. Consequently, both are quite surprised when the husband spends the night in jail and she cries, "Me, no understand!"

Other legal problems arise when international students are arrested for driving or vehicle-related violations, including special "modifications" to the car's body. Churches with an international ministry should also know about the employment laws governing international students. Often international students feel the crunch of having no money and consequently look for employment that violates their visas. Such violations can create a real problem and send them home in a heartbeat. It is also very beneficial to have a university professor or staff member in the church to assist international students with the many academic problems that surface and to mediate some of the difficult relationship issues that can arise.

THE INTERNATIONAL CHURCH— FOREIGN LANGUAGE

Sometimes the local church will need to consider starting an international church under the umbrella of the church to meet the special needs and interests of a particular international segment. For instance, if the college town has a large number of Chinese, Koreans, Japanese, or Spanish-speaking students, it may be wise to consider having worship services conducted in their language and culture. Starting an international church should be considered when the language barrier is hindering outreach to a good portion of the international community. In this case, the goal should be to have a separate international church for this group that is integrated as much as possible with the overall program of the English-speaking church. If there is a large international community with permanent residents and a professional base that could support a church-planting project, the long-term goal would be for the international church to become independent. However, in many cases, there is not the financial base available in the college town to plant an independent church. In that case, the international church is a subdivision of the English-speaking local church. This organization's structure would be the following:

The Lord Jesus Christ—"The Head of the Body, the Church" (Col. 1:18)

The Senior Pastor as the Undershepherd of the Local Church

| The International Pastor, Pastor/Missionary, or Director of the International Church |
| The International Deacon(s) and International Officers |
| The International Church Family—"doing the work of the ministry" (Eph. 4:12) |

The senior pastor of the English-speaking church would be responsible for the oversight and the general direction of the international church. He would need to define clearly the roles of each in the organizational chart and the chain of command.

The international pastor would be delegated the authority and responsibility to shepherd and to micromanage the international church. Under his care would be the necessary officers to conduct the business matters of the church and the social aspects of the ministry. The international pastor could be an ordained pastor, a pastor/missionary, or a layman. It is justifiable to follow the same pastor/missionary model discussed in chapter three to put into place the proper leadership for the international ministry. The international ministry is clearly foreign missions at its finest. On the larger campuses this ministry is more than one full-time missionary can handle. The long-term goal of the church with a campus ministry is to have a full-time international pastor.

In addition to the international pastor, in due time deacons could be selected. It would be best to have these deacons serve on the same board as the deacons for the English-speaking church. The international deacon(s) would represent the people and physical needs of the international church.

As with any church, the goal of the leadership is to train the church family to carry on the work of the Great Commission. Such training is invaluable for international students who will return to their homelands. For example, the Chinese students will be able return to China knowing how the local church is to conduct its ministry. They can adapt what they have learned to establish house churches until the door of religious freedom is opened in China.

Combined services of the English-speaking church and the international church should be encouraged at least once each semester. Easter, the Fourth of July, and Christmas make excellent times to combine the services. An interpreter should be provided for such services. In addition, the overall church should observe the ordinances in the combined services, especially the ordinance of baptism. What an encouragement it is for all to see international students baptized. The Lord's Supper can be observed in both the combined and separated services. It is also important to integrate certain aspects of the overall church ministry with the international church. One of the greatest assets to the international church is the influence and interaction of the American Christians. There are many things the two groups can do together: for example, music recitals and mission trips.

However, the international church should have its own Sunday school program, children's church program, and weekly prayer meeting and Bible study. These services should be conducted in their native tongue or translated from English to their native tongue. One good topic to teach to the international church is creation vs. evolution, as the vast majority of international students will be evolutionists when they come to America. They are very interested in learning of creation science, especially when it is presented by Christian scientists, engineers, or other professionals. In addition, because Christian music is one of the greatest vehicles to teach theology to the international students of all ages, the international ministry needs to focus on good Christian music and eventually develop an international choir.

To meet the special needs of the international church, the church should schedule family seminars and retreats as well as annual revival meetings and mission trips. Any Chinese students should be challenged to take a mission team into America's Chinatowns and preach the gospel.

The international student is a blessed addition to any campus mission team or testimony service and should be involved when pioneering a campus ministry on another college campus. A means of making Christians aware of the unique opportunity to reach the world through campus ministries is to conduct a radio broadcast about the unique opportunities of the international ministry. The program could be called "Focus on a Foreigner."

CHRISTIAN LITERATURE IN FOREIGN LANGUAGES

The American Christian should learn about the basic elements of each of the major world religions, such as Buddhism, Hinduism, and Islam, and learn the "dos" and "don'ts" of each group. Also, they should try to learn a few words in the native language of the people to whom they are ministering. Even just saying "hello" or "thank you" in their language will go a long way in building a relationship. If the Christian is ministering to the Chinese, C. H. Kang's book *Discovery of Genesis* and Samuel Wang's book *God and the Ancient Chinese* illustrate various biblical truths found in the picture language of the Chinese. The gospel can be presented in a captivating fashion using Chinese words such as "righteousness," which is a picture of a lamb over the personal pronoun "I," or the word "come," which is a picture of a cross with two men stationed on each side with one looking to the cross and the other away. It is very easy to challenge them to "come" to the cross and be like the one who looks to Jesus for salvation. The word "temptation" is a picture of a woman eating fruit with a serpent nearby. The list goes on of gospel pictures in the Chinese language.

In presenting the gospel to an international student, the Christian should follow the pattern of Paul in Athens in Acts 17. One of the most beneficial things someone can do for an international student is to give him a Bible in his language or, better yet, a Bible with his language on one side and English on the other. Gospel tapes in their language or the Bible on tape in their language are effective tools. The church should also have a supply of gospel tracts, literature, and videos in various languages readily available for distribution. The written testimonies of international students have an impact on fellow international students. In no way should the church downplay the role of literature in winning the lost. In 1959 John Mendow was witnessing to a member of the Liberation Army. The member of the Red Army snapped at Mendow and said, "You American missionaries are fools." Mendow quickly asked, "Why?" The answer that came back was "Because of your methods [open-air meetings]. Why don't you give them some literature [which would arouse their curiosity and they would go home and read it]?" The soldier continued by saying,

> You missionaries have been in China for over 100 years but you have not won China for your Christ. There are still uncounted millions that have never heard the name of your God. Nor do they know anything about your Christianity. We communists have been in China less than 10 years, but there is no such thing as a Chinese who has not heard the name of Stalin or who knows nothing of Communism. What you missionaries have failed to do in 100 years, we communists have done in 10. Now let me tell you how you failed. You preach by speaking; you attract crowds by building churches, schools, hospitals, and orphanages. But we communists have printed our message and spread literature over all China. We have told the people that Christianity is a religion for white people, that missionaries are spies of imperialist countries, and that Jesus Christ is merely an invention of capitalism, but our ideas have been imprinted in the hearts of people through propaganda bulletins, newspapers, magazines, and pamphlets. Soon we will drive you out of China and we will do it by means of printed pages.[8]

---

[8]Ambassadors for Christ, *Mainland Chinese in America*, 98.

8

Outreach Methods for the Campus Ministry

First Corinthians 9:20–23 states,

> And unto the Jews I became as a Jew, that I might gain the Jews;
> to them that are under the law, as under the law, that I might
> gain them that are under the law; to them that are without law,
> as without law, (being not without law to God, but under the law
> to Christ,) that I might gain them that are without law. To the
> weak became I as weak, that I might gain the weak: I am made
> all things to all men, that I might by all means save some. And
> this I do for the gospel's sake, that I might be partaker thereof
> with you.

Evangelist Bob Jones, Sr., used to preach, "Evangelistic unction
makes orthodoxy function."[1] The name of the game for any ministry
should be evangelism: outreach! The heart of the campus ministry is
to reach collegians for Christ's kingdom. Although this chapter emphasizes methodology, more important than all of these methods is
the message that Jesus saves! Methods are simply means by which
Christians put themselves in a position to present the gospel to the
unsaved. Christ used an array of methods in revealing Himself to
sinners, and so should Christians. The followers of Christ will have
a full tackle box to use in fishing for men.

---

[1]Bob Jones III, "Bob Jones Sr.'s Educational Philosophy," *Balance*, September
2001, 2.

SURVEYS

Surveys can be useful for getting some contact when the church is just starting a campus ministry. Once the campus ministry gets rolling, the ministry will have more contacts to follow up with than it can handle; but at first this tool can generate some one-on-one or small-group Bible studies. Regardless of the survey's topic, additional questions need to be asked regarding the student's interest in having a Bible study with someone from the campus ministry; these additional questions are the trigger for follow-up.

The campus ministry should conduct the surveys on campus at high-traffic locations, such as the post office and cafeterias. Inevitably, when doing surveys, workers will have opportunities to witness to someone and leave him a gospel tract and information about the campus ministry and church. When the survey is complete, ethically the survey results need to be published, perhaps in the school's student newspaper, which is a great venue for advertising or for submitting articles.

ONE-ON-ONE EVANGELISTIC BIBLE STUDIES

Almost all corporate campus meetings, outreaches, international dinners, surveys, and other activities include an invitation for the student to have a one-on-one soulwinning Bible study. Such Bible studies are a very informal method of campus evangelism. Many students who would not attend the weekly meeting or the services of the local church will agree to a Bible study. An individual or small-group study provides a relaxed atmosphere that encourages interaction and questions from participating students. Studies can be led by staff workers, interns, extension workers, or student leaders within the campus ministry.

Those people teaching the Bible studies need to be trained to use a soulwinning Bible study. One such study geared especially for college students is *The Ploughman's Sower Series*, a four-lesson study on the Gospel of John. This series is described in greater detail in chapter nine. Most students are willing to meet for a four-week Bible study. In many ways the students are like Nicodemus, who want to come to Jesus at night. Students who are saved can later use the same Bible study materials in conducting Bible studies with their friends. The small-group Bible studies are one of the "feeder" ministries into the weekly corporate meeting on campus and/or the local church.

THE WEEKLY MEETING

The weekly meeting on campus is the "bread and butter" meeting for all campus ministries that are structurally divorced from a local church. For them, this meeting is an all-or-nothing meeting. This is their church service; it is a major measuring stick as to how successful their organization is. The weekly meeting can be used to evangelize, to disciple, and to train leadership. For the campus ministry based out of the local church, the weekly meeting is important but not all-important, because it is just one of the ministry's many campus opportunities. The local-church-based campus ministry determines its "success" by students being saved, baptized, and participating in a local church ministry. Because of this philosophy, all campus outreaches have the ultimate goal of seeing students involved in the local church. The weekly meeting on campus needs to be at a convenient time and place for the students. There is much competition amongst the various groups for meeting places and times. Practically every night of the week there will be an organization meeting. Tuesdays and Thursdays seem to be the best nights, with Tuesday slightly better than Thursday because Thursday night often begins the weekend partying.

The weekly meeting should last approximately one hour and include prayer requests, singing, testimonies, and a Bible study. This meeting can be lighter in spirit and can be benefited by adding skits and other icebreakers. This is the meeting to which group members can invite new students. Typically the topics taught are of great interest to the student, and the students enjoy the fellowship.

The weekly meeting is not as critical for the group's faithful students because they are being fed at church on Sunday and on Wednesday night. However, they should use the meeting as an evangelistic tool and invite their friends who may go home on the weekends or who would not be as likely to attend a church service as they would a meeting on campus. The best way to promote this meeting is by word of mouth, although it also needs to be advertised.

THE MONTHLY OR SEMESTER SPECIAL LECTURE OR SPEAKER

Once a month or once a semester there should be a big push to get students out to the weekly meeting when there is a special speaker or topic that will be addressed. This meeting should be held at the same time as the weekly campus meeting but may need to be moved to a larger lecture hall, depending on the topic and anticipated attendance. Topics that draw students usually deal with controversy (e.g., abortion, AIDS, war, or homosexuality), creation vs. evolution, prophecy, or human-interest stories. At these meetings, as with all meetings, visitor cards are handed out. At the end of this meeting, the campus worker should give an invitation for the students to trust Christ and/or give the opportunity for the students to respond by stating their interest in a one-on-one Bible study.

This meeting could also be conducted outside in the form of an open-air evangelistic service. If the organization requests permission, the university will usually allow meetings to be held in the outdoor amphitheaters or other areas on campus. For open-air meetings, the campus ministry will want to arrange for special music, as loud and as tasteful as possible, and a good public-address system or an acoustically designed amphitheater. There will no doubt be a crowd that gathers. Evangelistic messages need to be shorter, and several speakers may want to take time preaching to the students. Counselors should be stationed around the front to keep hecklers from throwing tomatoes and to assist those who are seeking spiritual counsel. Such evangelistic meetings need to be revived on the campuses!

CHRISTIAN LITERATURE DISTRIBUTION

At the beginning of the fall and spring semesters, the campus ministry should plan a massive mail-out campaign during which the group mails to every student a brochure of the church and campus ministry information, including the events and van pick-up locations for church. Most importantly, in each of these brochures the group should include either a gospel tract or a gospel presentation on the brochure. This information is included in the fall and spring mail-outs. Every student who has a campus post office box will have two opportunities during the school year to read how he can be saved from his sins. Another goal would be to distribute a New Testament to every student.

There are many other opportunities for distributing Christian literature through the year. For example, at the start of each year, some universities schedule a day for the campus organizations to promote their clubs and ministries. The church-based campus ministry can use this day to conduct surveys, distribute tracts and information about the ministry, and solicit individual Bible studies. Great opportunities for tract distribution are also available at most college athletic events. At some larger schools, group members could hand out more than 50,000 tracts at the football stadium. A bolder approach would be to rent one of the planes that circle the stadium during the game and present a Bible phrase each quarter so that by the end of the game, everyone would have read the Romans Road over and over and over again. Rock concerts also provide great opportunities to distribute tracts. The most strategic location for distributing tracts is away from the stadium where Purple Floyd or the Rolling Pebbles may be imitating the prophets of Baal, near the port-o-johns. Usually there is a long line of people waiting to use the port-o-johns, which makes tract distribution very easy: one simply walks down the line. They can read the tract right there, and if they throw it on the ground, someone else will pick it up later. Or one may just tell some people to put the tract in their pocket and read it in the morning.

ACTIVITIES DESIGNED FOR OUTREACH

The campus ministry should design activities for evangelistic purposes, not simply to have fun. Chapter ten will address the campus calendar and scheduled activities and retreats that can be used for evangelistic purposes. For example, the ministry could have a Friday preaching night at the church at which four to eight male students each preach a short message. These students will benefit from their diligent study of the Bible in preparation for preaching, and they can invite their unsaved friends to hear them. In due time some of the "student preachers" will be asking the pastor for an application to the closest Bible college or seminary.

INVITING STUDENTS TO THE LOCAL CHURCH

Members of a campus ministry based out of a local church can invite students to the church to hear the gospel every week or can invite students to special evangelistic services or revival meetings. Opportunities for students to hear the gospel abound with a local church that has a campus ministry. The home church is the campus ministry's "bread and butter"!

SPORTS OUTREACHES

Sports outreaches, which may be a novel idea to some and a concern to others, are one of the most effective means of gathering college students in order to preach the gospel to them.

The apostle Paul sought to win the Jews and Gentiles by various means. He would adopt the best means, based on their backgrounds and interests, to gain them for Christ. However, in the process of winning people to the Lord, Paul was sensitive not to violate a biblical principle. And despite his changing methods, Paul's gospel message never changed.

Today, Christians need creative "means" to "save some."[2] One such "means" is sports outreaches because of the great interest in sports. Ninety-four percent of Americans watch, read about, or participate in athletics on a monthly basis. This phenomenal percentage is rivaled in almost all parts of the world. Sports outreaches target this large interest group with the gospel. Many people who may not be able to be reached by any other means can be gained for Christ through sports outreaches.

---

[2]1 Cor. 9:22.

From the apostle Paul's writings, it is quite obvious that he was familiar with sports and had no reservation about using athletic metaphors to illustrate important spiritual truths. Although Paul used a wide variety of metaphors, he used athletic metaphors frequently, using only military and agricultural metaphors more frequently. In addition, in twelve of Paul's thirteen epistles, he used no less than thirty-three athletic metaphors to illustrate spiritual truths. Christians would be wise to learn from Paul's effective example and use sports today as a means of communicating spiritual truths.

Christians can not only use the language of sports, but can also use sports as a means to gather unsaved people together so that they can hear the gospel! Unlike in Paul's day, when athletes competed nude, events were dedicated to the Greek god Zeus, and some events were barbaric and not appropriate for a believer's endorsement, Christians today can watch and/or participate in most sporting events without violating their conscience. Hence the birth of sports outreaches. Sports outreaches are simply Christians inviting students or other people to participate in a sporting event that has the expressed intention, given to all parties, that the main event will be the preaching of the Word of God.

9

DISCIPLESHIP GOALS

THE PRODUCT OF
DISCIPLESHIP

T he spiritual goal of the Christian is to be like Christ, to be conformed to His image. Romans 8:29 states, "For whom he did fore-
know, he also did predestinate to be conformed to the image of his
Son, that he might be the firstborn among many brethren." The
blessing is that God has predetermined for every believer to be just
like His Son; this will take place at glorification. However, prior to
glorification, the justified believer in this life has entered the process
of sanctification. The present goal is for the believer to practically
live in light of his spiritual position in Christ and to look forward
to the promise that he will be like Christ. The aim of discipleship,
then, is for each Christian to strive to be Christlike. This means
a Christian's spiritual children and spiritual grandchildren should
look like Christ.

THE PROOF OF DISCIPLESHIP

The heart goal in discipleship is for Christians to "love the Lord
thy God with all thy heart, and with all thy soul, and with all thy
strength, and with all thy mind; and thy neighbour as thyself."[1] This
goal presents the content of the Christian's message that he needs
to "commit to faithful men."[2] Therefore, the discipler's job is very
simple: all he has to do is teach his disciples two commandments.

---

[1] Luke 10:27.
[2] 2 Tim. 2:2.

Then his disciples are to teach their disciples just two commandments. Once these two commandments are complied with in his life and in the lives of his disciples and their disciples, his discipleship is complete.

The Procedure for Discipleship

Second Timothy 2:2 states, "And the things that thou hast heard of me among many witnesses, the same commit thou to faithful men, who shall be able to teach others also." This verse stresses the methodological goal of discipleship: to train someone so well that he will "be able to teach others also." Biblical discipleship, then, involves three tiers. There are things that the discipler/trainer needs to know. This knowledge, then, is to be passed down from the trainer/discipler to the next tier, those being discipled. Then the person who is discipled is to teach those of the third tier. The real test of whether one is a biblical discipler is whether his converts are teaching others. If the knowledge committed to faithful Christians stops at the second tier, the discipler has fallen short in his discipling. One has not truly discipled a person until he sees that person teaching someone else. Once this happens, the person on the first tier has completed his methodological goal with that person. This means that each "generation" of Christians should have spiritual grandchildren. All Christians should be grandparents!

To summarize what discipleship means is as simple as 1-2-3.

1 Example to be like

2 Commandments to keep

3 Levels to commit to the goal of one person to be like and two commandments to keep.

The Place of Discipleship: The Local Church

In the last fifty years campus ministries have been pioneers in organizing discipleship materials and a game plan on how these materials are to be used. For example, the old-school Navigators had a real zeal for Bible study and memory work, which was encouraged by some excellent discipleship materials. The major concern about their materials was not what they wrote and taught but what they ignored and omitted, such as the doctrine of the church and the doctrine of separation. As a result of these oversights, the Navigators have gone so far that they have yoked up with the church on the "seven mountains."[3] The doctrine of separation is the wall that keeps the world out and the believer pure. If there is no biblical wall being put in place, it is just a matter of time before a ministry will be swallowed up in worldliness and compromise.

The beauty of a campus ministry rooted in a local church is the presence of "many witnesses" (2 Timothy 2:2). The campus worker is not the only "witness" or teacher, for there are many people serving the Lord and assisting in the sanctification process. The local church also provides further instruction in the Word of God on topics that new Christians need for growth. Not everything hinges on the one trainer, as there is an entire church family that the Lord uses to encourage the new converts. The Lord has wisely designed the local church to be the headquarters for discipleship.

THE PLURALITY OF DISCIPLESHIP

Most Christians need some structure and some direction as to how to disciple someone else, particularly because most Christians were never personally discipled themselves. Discipleship should be conducted on a personal level and corporate level, with the local church being part of "the many witnesses" in the discipleship process. If there is just one-on-one discipleship, it is easier to breed the discipler's weaknesses into the next spiritual generation. In addition, if personal discipleship is overemphasized, the discipler may become overly possessive. For example, members of parachurch groups often speak of their "disciple" and are so possessive of the person that they are working with that it seems they would be offended if someone said boo to their disciple! Balance and safeguards against these problems are built in when the discipler engages in corporate discipleship. However, if there is only corporate discipleship (e.g.,

---

[3]Rev. 17:9.

Sunday school, worship services, retreats), there can be many gaps in the discipleship process due to a lack of interaction, participation, personal accountability, and times for questions and answers. Although this chapter stresses one-on-one discipleship because it is greatly omitted in fundamentalist circles, the mainframe for discipleship is the local church environment. Discipleship that runs parallel to the local church or does not funnel into the local church is mutant discipleship and will create spiritual dwarfs.

THE PRACTICE OF DISCIPLESHIP

Paul "committed" certain teachings to "faithful men." The question is, what did he transmit so that today's Christians can do the same? It is obvious that Paul's epistles summarize his teaching. Certainly the Pauline epistles should be "commit[ed] . . . to faithful men."[4] It also would be a safe step of hermeneutics to state that in general the discipler is committing to "faithful men" the Word of God. Therefore, having each new Christian read the entire Bible, probably beginning with the New Testament, would be an appropriate goal to include in the scope of discipleship. Another question would be "What teachings of the Bible and practices would be most important to communicate first to a new convert?" This study will address the question, "Where should one begin in the discipleship process with a new convert?"

The Ploughman's Harvest and *Treasure Series*

Regardless of what tools are used in discipleship, essential topics to cover with a new Christian include assurance of salvation, baptism, the church, Bible study, prayer, and soulwinning. Therefore, when someone is saved in the Cross Impact Ministries (formerly called the Spurgeon Foundation Campus Ministries), three documents are put into his hands:

The Bible

The Ploughman's Harvest Series (a six-lesson discipleship study book)

The Ploughman's Treasure Series (The Gospel of Matthew)

---

[4]2 Tim. 2:2.

The First Discipleship Appointment
Within the Cross Impact Campus Ministries, the discipler meets with the convert and reviews with him the Bible, *The Ploughman's Harvest Series*, and *The Ploughman's Treasure Series*. The new convert is then assigned two Bible study goals: to complete the first lesson in *The Ploughman's Harvest Series* on "Assurance of Salvation," which can be completed at one sitting or over the course of the week, and to read one chapter from the Bible each day, beginning in Matthew chapter one. It is important for the discipler to help the convert immediately establish the habit of daily Bible reading. He needs daily food! *The Ploughman's Treasure Series*, a devotional guide, can help the convert gain this food. As he reads one chapter a day, he is to respond to the three study guide suggestions: to list any verses that were a blessing to him, to write down any questions from the chapter, and to list any verses in the chapter that relate to a particular theme he is interested in, such as prayer, prophecy, or child-rearing. (This last response area can be introduced to the convert at a later date.) Using this method forces the convert to read the Bible with purpose. Included in the back of *The Ploughman's Treasure Series* is a place to list any prayer requests. Ask the convert to write the prayer requests closest to his heart in this section and to pray each day that the Lord will answer his prayer requests. This section of the *Treasure Series* will become a prayer journal which can later be transferred to *The Ploughman's Journal* when it is introduced.

The discipler can encourage the new convert to attend church with him as well at this appointment. Circumstances will vary, and the discipler will need to be sensitive as to how far he can go with the new convert. Babies have a hard time even crawling; the discipler should not expect a babe in Christ to take big steps. Discipleship is "line upon line,"[5] so he should be patient. The very fact that he has directed the convert to the Word of God and to a time in prayer is foundational to everything that flows from the Christian life. The discipler's goal is to see the convert's relationship with Christ develop. If the convert's relationship with the Head develops, that convert will be rightly related to the body, the church, in due time.

---

[5]Isa. 28:10.

Regardless of whether the convert commits to coming to church, set up the next discipleship appointment with him, usually for a week later. In some cases, the meetings may need to be more frequent. It is best to schedule sixty to ninety minutes for each discipleship appointment. The discipler should state that goal and stick to it unless it is obvious God wants him to stay longer. The point is to be very respectful of the convert's time and for him to be appreciative of the discipler's.

During the week, the discipler should give the convert a call and see how he is doing on his assignments. It is also imperative for the discipler to work through lesson one of *The Ploughman's Harvest Series* and to study the first seven chapters in Matthew to be prepared for any of his questions. The discipler may want to list in the second section all the verses that he has questions on and then study to find answers to these questions. He may also want to use the third block to study a particular theme in Matthew for his own devotions. It also wouldn't hurt for him to list any blessings in the first section. It is obvious by the tone of the last three sentences that the discipler needs to be walking with God and working too!

Appointment to Cover Assurance of Salvation
The main goal of this meeting is for the person being discipled to know that he is truly saved and that he knows it is based on scriptural reasons. The lesson is designed to address the reasons people struggle with this knowledge as well as how to remedy the problem. If the discipler senses that the person understands that he is saved by the grace of God, encourage him to tell at least one person during the next week that he was recently saved.

The discipler should also ask how his daily reading from the book of Matthew went and whether he has any blessings to share or questions to ask. The discipler should not be surprised if he did not read his Bible every day or if he has not written much, or anything, in his devotional guide. Instead, he should encourage him to start where he left off during the next week; he should also encourage him to begin the journey of reading a minimum of one chapter of the Bible every day of his life. If he has blessings, the discipler should let him share them and sincerely "ooh" and "ah" with him! Obviously, the discipler can share what the Lord has been teaching him in the Scriptures during each of these meetings as well. If he has questions from his reading, the discipler should try to answer them. If he does not readily have an answer, he should tell the convert that he does not know but that for the next meeting he will try to have an answer.

As the discipler closes the study, he should ask whether the convert has any prayer requests that were answered that week and whether he has anything for which he would like the discipler to pray. Afterward the discipler should simply pray and then confirm the next week's meeting and assignments, which would be to complete lesson two and to continue with his reading in Matthew. Again, he can gently invite the person to church. Also, sometime during the next week, he should call the person to see how he is doing. Finally, the discipler should pray for the convert daily.

Appointment to Cover Baptism

The study on baptism is critical for the convert to understand and to obey. At the heart of this lesson is the importance of a Christian's publicly confessing that he is God's child. When the discipler meets with the person on this occasion, he should ask him whom he told during the week that he was saved and what the person's response was. The person who is saved will understand the reality of Romans 10:11, "For the scripture saith, Whosoever believeth on him shall not be ashamed."

For this lesson the discipler needs to be aware of the many challenges that surround the topic of baptism and be aware that some cults teach the heresy of baptismal regeneration. It is amazing how Satan sends his vultures after the babes in Christ to confuse and deceive them. The author has compiled a study that deals with the seven baptismal passages which the cults twist to teach that baptism is needed for salvation. This study could be given to the new convert at this point for him to have available in his files.

The goal of this lesson is for the new convert to know the spiritual meaning of baptism, to understand the biblical pattern of when and how a person should be baptized, and to obey Scripture and follow that pattern. The Bible is very clear that baptism is to take place after one's conversion; immersion is strongly implied. After reviewing this study with the convert, the discipler should ask him what he thinks of getting baptized by immersion. If he understands that this is what he needs to do and desires at this point to obey, the discipler should reassure him of his good decision and tell him that he will be glad to meet with him and the pastor to arrange for a time for his baptism. He needs to ask, "What doth hinder you from being baptized?"[6] He should seek to find out the root problem and graciously address it. If the convert continues to resist, the discipler should simply tell him that he will be praying for him on this point and transition to his Scripture reading for the week.

The discipler should try to answer his questions from his Scripture reading and ask him to share blessings from the Word and from his prayer life. At the end of this session, the discipler should pray for him and his requests. Regardless of whether the convert is going to be immediately baptized, the discipler should have him write down "the need of being baptized" in his prayer journal in the back of *The Treasure Series* booklet. Then he should assign him his next lesson and confirm the next appointment. The discipler should call him that week to see how he is doing and should pray for him daily.

If the convert decided to be baptized immediately, the discipler should contact the pastor after this meeting and set up a time for the baptism. The new convert should inform his family and friends of his upcoming baptism so that they can attend the service if possible. If the discipler is working with children and youth, he needs to get written permission from his parents or guardians before baptizing the new convert.

Appointment to Cover the Church

The goal of the third appointment is to cover the importance of attending, joining, and getting involved in a good, fundamental, Bible-believing church. In addition to teaching what a good church is, this lesson seeks to safeguard the new convert against the Charismatic movement and its erroneous teaching on tongues. Each lesson has a deliberate side path to take if the discipler needs to take

---

[6]Allusion to Acts 8:36.

it to reinforce something that he senses might be a hindrance to the new convert. This lesson could raise many questions and curiosities about the fundamental church and other denominations. The goal of this lesson is not to run down other churches but to point the new believer in Christ to the type of church Christ approves of, based on Scripture. For additional information on the type of church Christ approves of, there is a supplemental study available on Christ's assessment of the seven churches in the book of Revelation. In this study both the pros and cons of the seven churches are emphasized. Obviously the goal for every Christian is to be in a church that Christ approves of and that has the qualities Christ commends. Ideally the new convert will want to join the discipler's church, which implies he has been or will be baptized.

It would be helpful for the discipler to give a copy of his church's constitution to the new convert during this appointment. Also, as he covers the section in the study on tithing, it might be helpful for the discipler to have a church budget on hand to explain how the Lord's money is used. He should also give to the convert any other information on the church that would be helpful. The discipler should ask the convert to read the constitution during the next week and ask him to write "the Lord's will regarding which church to join" in his prayer journal. He should also ask the convert to pray about this matter and to ask God for His leading and timing on the issue. At the end of this session, the discipler will want to pray for the convert about joining a church and, if still necessary, about being baptized.

Throughout the lesson the convert may wish to discuss a variety of topics, such as the Lord's Supper, the church's music standard, ministries to get involved in, the choir, or the missions program. The discipler should highlight what he thinks is important and stress the importance of church attendance and how the growing Christian will desire to be in each of the church services. The long-term goal for the convert is to attend Sunday school, the Sunday morning service, the Sunday evening service, and the Wednesday night prayer meeting. Also, the seed is being planted as to which areas the new convert could get involved in. It is going to be critical for any new convert to be given some spiritual responsibilities and to get to work in the Lord's vineyard.

The discipler should review the convert's reading of Matthew and seek to answer his questions. Then he should close in prayer. The discipler should call him during the week to see how he is doing and daily pray for him. These initial decisions by the young convert—to be baptized, to start attending church, to join, and even to begin tithing—are enormous steps for one to take and clearly evidence the Spirit of God at work when one submits his will to the Master's.

Appointment to Cover the Topic of Bible Study
The goal of the fourth lesson is to encourage the new believer to keep hearing, reading, studying, meditating on, and obeying the Bible. This lesson will allow the discipler to get caught up on the blessings and questions from the convert's reading from Matthew. If he has been flawless in his devotions, he has just completed reading his first book in the Bible. At this point the discipler will want to encourage him to continue reading one chapter a day.

If the discipler anticipates his having completed *The Ploughman's Treasure Series* on Matthew, he should bring with him the next booklet in *The Ploughman's Treasure Series*, which covers the Gospel of Mark. When introducing *The Ploughman's Treasure Series* on Mark, he may want to suggest a theme for the convert to study in each chapter and have him record verses relating to that theme in the third section of each day's study. If he is following the daily reading schedule and recording the verses that especially spoke to his heart and listing questions, he is beginning to learn how to feed himself spiritual food. For further Bible study or reading, a suggested reading list and commentary selection is available for his files. This also would be a good time for the discipler to introduce the convert to a Bible concordance and other helpful study tools. He may also want to introduce the "Cost of Discipleship" memory program at this point as well as *The Ploughman's Journal*, which are discussed later in this chapter.

Also at this session the discipler should ask if he has made a decision on baptism or the church. He should not be pushy but should make the convert accountable on these issues. As with each session, the discipler should ask how his daily Bible reading is going and seek to answer his questions from the reading. Before leaving, the discipler should confirm the next appointment and assignment and close by praying with the convert. During the next week he should call the convert to see how he is doing and daily pray for him.

Appointment to Cover Prayer

The goal of this session is the study what the Bible has to teach regarding prayer and to answer any of the convert's questions on this topic. This is a good time for the discipler to review the convert's prayer requests in *The Ploughman's Treasure Series* and to encourage him to note God's promises on prayer as he does his daily reading. The subject of prayer is an excellent first topic for the convert to study. By this time, the convert will most likely be ready to start his reading in Mark, if he has not started already. He should have *The Ploughman's Treasure Series* on Mark. The discipler should suggest to him that as he starts this second Gospel, he should look for passages on prayer and note them in the daily reading section (e.g., Mark 1:35 could be written down for chapter one). His *Treasure Series* would then be divided into these three sections for each chapter that he is reading:

1. Blessings from the passage on any subject
2. Questions from the reading
3. References to prayer in the chapter

Once again, the discipler should review the convert's Bible reading and seek to answer his questions from the reading. At the end of this meeting, the discipler will want to pray for the convert, highlighting some of the prayer requests from his prayer list. The discipler should also confirm the next appointment and the assignment to complete the last chapter of *The Ploughman's Harvest Series.*

The discipler can also challenge the new convert to find two Christians whom he could call at any time to serve as his intercessory prayer partners. In addition, he can challenge him to come to prayer meeting and pray with these prayer partners on Wednesday nights. Prayer is going to be essential for the convert's growth. The young Christian needs to be urged to start his day early in the Word and in prayer. An example of a young believer's desire to spend quality time with the Lord is seen in Dawson Trotman's journal. The founder of the Navigators wrote in his journal, "Slept till 7:00

a.m. Shame! Because of this I must begin the day with but a few minutes of prayer. This is sin."[7] Dawson Trotman recognized the need of establishing an early, consistent time in the day to seek the Lord in prayer.

Appointment to Cover Soulwinning
This session completes *The Ploughman's Harvest Series,* which ends on a very important note: soulwinning. There are several goals for this appointment. At the end of this study, the discipler wants the convert to understand that soulwinning is not just an option but is mandated by the King and to know the elements of the gospel and various ways to scatter the seed. The growing Christian will want to tell others about Christ. The discipler should challenge the new convert to make a list of people who he knows are unsaved, which may include his family and friends. He should then ask the convert to pray for each person by name and seek to witness to them by giving to them his testimony of salvation and/or by giving them a gospel tract or other literature.

As in each discipleship meeting the discipler should review the new convert's daily Bible reading, asking him to share the blessings from the Bible and his questions. The discipler will also need to assess how far the convert is in his reading and see if he needs any additional guides from *The Ploughman's Treasure Series.* These simple and inexpensive guides cover the entire New Testament. The discipler should encourage the new Christian to maintain the lifetime habit of reading a minimum of one chapter of the Bible a day and state that he will continue to touch base with him on his reading and will continue to seek to answer any questions he has.

Because this is the last study in *The Ploughman's Harvest Series,* the discipler will need to ask the person if he would like to continue to meet and if he would be interested in being trained in using *The Ploughman's Journal,* a discipleship tool discussed below, and in the five steps of the soulwinner's "Gospel Go Plan." If there is good interest in continuing, the discipler should confirm the next appointment and give the convert *The Ploughman's Journal* and *The*

---

[7]Skinner, *DAWS,* 51.

Ploughman's Manual, telling him to read *The Ploughman's Manual* for the next appointment.

The Ploughman's Journal and *The Ploughman's Manual*

At the next meeting the discipler will review *The Ploughman's Manual*, which describes how to use the five sections in *The Ploughman's Journal*. These sections are named after titles used by Charles Haddon Spurgeon.

The first section of *The Ploughman's Journal* is called "Morning and Evening." This section is laid out like "The Ploughman's Treasure Series" and is to be used in an identical fashion. The new convert is already quite familiar with this Bible study approach for his devotions. Now his continued studies for one year will be nicely kept in *The Ploughman's Journal*.

The second section, called "Faith's Checkbook," is simply a prayer journal; again this will look familiar to the new convert because he has been following the same format in the back of *The Ploughman's Treasure Series*. The discipler should ask the convert to unify his prayer journal by transcribing his prayer requests from *The Ploughman's Treasure Series* to this section of *The Ploughman's Journal*.

In the third section, called the "Soulwinner," he should record the names of his unsaved friends and family and his soulwinning activity. Also in *The Ploughman's Manual* is a soulwinning plan, called the "Gospel Go Plan," which will be somewhat new to the convert and will serve as the heart of this phase of his training. By this time in his Christian experience, he needs to be equipped to win people to Christ. Such tools are introduced in more detail in this section of *The Ploughman's Journal*.

The fourth section is called "Lectures to My Students" and is to be used for taking notes of sermons, Sunday school messages, Bible studies, and other messages. The section also provides a nice filing system for taking and keeping notes. The long-term goal is for each Christian to have a filing system and/or library that assists him in keeping track of materials that relate textually (i.e., separate folders for all sixty-six books of the Bible) to the Bible as well as topically (i.e., baptism, spiritual gifts, rapture, millennium, child-rearing).

The final section is called "The Sword and the Trowel." This section deals with an extensive memory program available for the new convert. *The Ploughman's Manual* instructs the believer on why to memorize and how to memorize. The new convert will be introduced to two memory packs: the C-Pack and the R-Pack. The topics in the C-Pack will be very familiar to the new convert, as the pack includes two verses each on assurance of salvation, baptism, the church, Bible study, prayer, and soulwinning. The R-Pack is a "beefed-up" Romans Road package that will be used in conjunction with his training in soulwinning.

At this meeting the discipler should challenge the new convert to continue having his daily devotions, now using the "Morning and Evening" section in *The Ploughman's Journal*, to transcribe his prayer journal and soulwinning concern list to the "Faith's Checkbook" and the "Soulwinner" sections respectively, to use the "Lectures to My Students" section in taking notes of the next sermon, and to begin memorizing the first two verses of the R-Pack (Romans 3:10 and Romans 3:23). It would be also good for him to reread the section on soulwinning in *The Ploughman's Manual*. Finally, the discipler should confirm the next appointment and pray with the convert. During the week, the discipler should call him to see how he is doing and pray for him daily.

Teaching "The Gospel Go Plan" for Soulwinning

In the weeks to come, the discipler will follow the section on soulwinning in *The Ploughman's Manual*. This process will include the new convert's memorizing the R-Pack (the Romans Road), writing out his conversion testimony, and practicing, with his trainer, the techniques of winning someone to Christ. The team will then transition from the "laboratory" to going out together to win souls. This is an exciting period for both the trainer and the trainee.

The Ploughman's Manual also includes further instruction on other methods in getting the gospel to the unsaved, including having an evangelistic Bible study using *The Ploughman's Sower Series*, which is discussed below.

The Ploughman's Sower Series

This study covers four conversion experiences in the Gospel of John. The four soulwinning studies deal with Nicodemus, the Samaritan woman at the well, the blind man, and Thomas. Each study is geared to win the person who is being worked with to Christ. Each study has a slightly different thrust. For instance, the first lesson will appeal to the religious, but lost, person. The second lesson will parallel the lifestyle of the immoral sinner. The third study deals with those who may be physically afflicted or those who do not fit in. The last study is more of an apologetic approach to the gospel that parallels Thomas's need to simply have more evidence before he would believe.

When the discipler is training the new convert to use these studies, he should assign one chapter a week and cover the material carefully so that the trainee is comfortable with the lessons and the essential points of each lesson. The goal is for the trainer and the trainee to engage in a personal Bible study with an unsaved person or with several interested seekers. The eventual goal is for the trainee to be able to teach evangelistic Bible studies on his own and to later teach someone else to conduct such studies.

The Discipleship Cycle

As the young Christian matures and begins to spiritually reproduce Christlikeness not only in his character but also in winning souls, it will be his responsibility "to teach others also" to the point that his converts are teaching "others also." The maturing young Christian can teach others by taking his converts through *The Ploughman's Harvest Series* and *The Ploughman's Treasure Series* and advancing them to the next level of training using *The Ploughman's Journal* and *The Ploughman's Manual*. As those on the second tier go through the cycle again, they are already familiar with *The Ploughman's Harvest Series* because they were discipled with it. Now they can take what they have learned and teach the next spiritual generation. This process, a "spiritual hydrological cycle," should continue without ever drying up.

Additional Bible Studies

Building with the Trowel Bible Doctrines Series (in process) —This is a series of studies on the major doctrines of the faith, which are important to cover with any new Christian.

The Creation Series—This series deals with the first eleven chapters of Genesis and provides clear teaching on the doctrine of creation while refuting the follies of evolution. This topic is of great interest to many and truly is foundational to the faith.

The Contender Series—This series deals with the issues of personal separation, separation from false teachers, and separation from disobedient believers. It is a helpful study for the young Christian seeking to gain discernment and to keep himself pure.

Changed into His Image (JourneyForth), by Dr. Jim Berg, is another excellent series that will assist the believer in becoming more like Christ.

10

CAMPUS MINISTRY ACTIVITIES, PLANNING THE CAMPUS CALENDAR, AND INVOLVEMENT GOALS

In planning for the campus ministry calendar, the campus worker should think first in terms of semesters (fall, spring, and summer, in that order) and then think in terms of months, then weeks. This chapter describes the various events, activities, fellowships, retreats, and mission trips of a typical school year and the planning required to minister primarily to the single undergraduate and graduate students.

At the close of each semester, the campus worker and the student officers should evaluate the semester and fine-tune plans for the next semester's calendar. The Sunday school teacher, faculty advisor, and other interested and involved workers with the campus ministry could also be included in this meeting. There should be several brainstorming meetings scheduled during the year for fresh ideas. In addition, each individual event should be evaluated by the campus worker and the officers immediately after its completion while it is fresh on their minds.

After determining the semester's schedule, the campus workers and student officers will need to begin making preparations. For example, some guest speakers will need to be lined up far in advance, and some of the calendar events will need months of planning and advance notice (e.g., reserving the gyms for the annual basketball outreach tournament, making arrangements with another fundamental church for the Spring Break mission trip).

FALL SEMESTER

Move-In Day

August kicks off the school year; students will be returning during the month. The university will declare a specific day on which they officially open the dormitories and campus apartments for students to return. On this day, plans should be made to greet new students and to assist them in moving in. Students involved in the campus ministry should be prepared with moving dollies, refreshments, and water to make a great first impression for the Lord on the students' first day. All a campus worker needs to say is, "We are from such-and-such campus ministry. Can we help move you in?" After moving things in from the students' cars, moving vans, and trucks, the workers should leave with them some literature on the campus ministry and the local church and invite them to the church. The most strategic area to target is the freshman housing areas, because these students have yet to establish any spiritual roots or friends and, if they are like most college students who are interested in churches or campus ministries, they will make their decision as to where they want to attend church in the first six weeks of the fall semester.

Mass Mail-Out

During the first two weeks of the semester, there should be a mass mail-out to all the students on campus with information about the campus ministry and its plans for the semester as well as information on the local church. The campus ministry should also include a clear gospel presentation and an invitation to the group's next large outreach event. It takes manpower to put together the many mailing units, but this can be a great time for students and church members to work together. A similar mass mail-out needs to be done at the start of the spring semester.

Campus Organizations Day

Each year at the beginning of the fall semester, the university designates a day and a place for all the student campus organizations to promote their organization. This is a great day to make new contacts and to establish some campus presence. A banner of the organization should be displayed, and the campus worker needs to have lots of information on the campus ministry ready for distribution. In addition, the campus ministry may want to display a sign-up list for those interested in having individual Bible studies.

A Semester Kick-Off (Rally-in-the-Valley) Conference/Retreat
A great way to kick off the school year is to have a retreat or rally scheduled around the college's opening-day football game. This event could last all weekend, with preaching and activities based at the local church. The campus ministry should invite not only students from the college but also members of other local college-career groups and campus ministries. The best combination is to invite college students from the opposing college who will be cheering on their team against the "home" team. This "rivalry" lends itself to a lot of fun and creates a lively environment for the conference. The conference would begin on Friday night and end with the Sunday morning service at the local church. Housing and meals would need to be arranged for the out-of-town guests. This is an exciting way to start the semester and will provide some new contacts.

The Weekly Campus Meeting
Each week of the semester, usually on Tuesday or Thursday, the campus ministry should hold a meeting on campus. The meetings could include singing, testimonies, prayer, skits, games, food, and discussions. There should be about fourteen such meetings each semester.

The theme for these meetings should be planned and advertised. Although the mass mail-out document highlighted these meetings, the campus ministry should have flyers available for students to use to invite their friends and should place some posters on the bulletin boards and kiosks of the campus, which typically requires having the poster approved by the university or student government.

The Monthly Evangelistic Service
Once a month during the time slot of the weekly campus meeting, the campus worker should schedule a special speaker, a film, a debate, or some other event. These meetings should be widely promoted and advertised.

Weekly Activities

The undergraduate students in particular need to be kept busy with fun activities with purpose. Normally the campus ministry will want to plan an activity for every weekend or for every other weekend. Some weeks this can be as simple as going bowling (how boring) or as elaborate as a progressive or a regressive dinner, which would involve a handful of families in the church. The student officers and other students should plan much of these activities, with supervision from the campus pastor (worker). There should be a gospel challenge given at each planned activity that officially represents the campus organization, and students should regularly invite unsaved students to the activities. Each month, the campus ministry should plan one major activity that is exciting or unusual enough to draw unsaved students (e.g., whitewater rafting, horseback riding, ski retreat).

Visitation and Bible Study Times

The active campus ministry must have a very zealous visitation team as there are going to be many contacts who will need to be followed up. These contacts will come from those who visited church or the weekly campus meeting, the organizations day or any surveys which were conducted, sports outreaches, the International Day/Dinner, referrals, or other means.

The campus worker or other members will also need to start small evangelistic Bible studies with students who have shown interest. In addition, the campus ministry will need to disciple students who know the Lord. These activities require coordination and a massive amount of time and energy. Although there should be a set time for visitation, the Bible studies will need to be conducted at the convenience of the student and the teacher/trainer/discipler.

Wednesday Night Dinners Prior to the Prayer Meeting

To encourage student attendance at the mid-week prayer meeting, families in the church can host students for a meal prior to the service. If a family gives students an open invitation, the students will come for a good meal and for the family environment. Although this ministry requires a lot of work by the host families, it will be eternally worth the investment.

Church families could also invite students to join them for a meal after one of the Sunday services. Or students in the campus ministry could invite their contacts and other visitors to join them before or after a service for a cookout or for a meal at a restaurant. Everyone has to eat, so why not follow Matthew's banquet pattern[1] for sinners and invite them so that they can be introduced to Christ?

Sunday Night Testimony Times
Once a month or once a semester, the campus ministry should have a short service following an evening service at which students have a mini-singspiration and present testimonies about the Lord's work in their lives. Several families in the church or the deacons could be invited to this informal meeting. Pizza always makes this a well-attended meeting.

Sports Outreach Tournaments and Events
During the fall semester there will be the potential for the campus ministry to host a handful of different sports outreaches. The best events for the fall seem to be soccer (short-field, six-on-six), volleyball (four-on-four), flag football, and a 5K race. Such outreaches have been described in chapter eight. The 5K Fun Run is especially a "hoot" if "Sea Turtle" running rules are used. This run/walk works nicely with a fall missions conference. In addition, American students may want to form a team to participate in the annual international soccer outreach tournament, which is held in the fall.

Fall Break Retreat or Mission Trip
The Fall Break presents an extended opportunity to do something with the college students, such as a retreat or mission trip. Typically, Fall Break is four days long, including the weekend. More will be said about mission trips under "Spring Break Mission Trip" later in this chapter.

---

[1]Matt. 9:9–13.

Deputation Services with Campus Missionary

If the campus worker is a missionary, he will need to visit his supporting churches at times as well as solicit additional missionary support. During the school year especially, he should stay within his state or region for such meetings and solicit support from outside of the area during the summer when the campus ministry slows down. At such meetings during the school year, it is a tremendous blessing to all parties to have college students join the campus worker and sing and/or give testimonies.

If the church has a fully supported college pastor, he should still hold Sunday evening or Wednesday evening services at churches within the state about three or four times each semester. These meetings will encourage more Christians in the state to pray for the campus ministry and will create a system for church members to give the campus ministry new contacts by providing names of students who are attending the various state schools.

Christmas Programs and/or Banquet

December is a very busy time for the student, and campus workers need to be sensitive about the students' need to study, especially during finals. Finals are usually the first or second week of the month, and when they turn in that last test, students are generally off the campus and running home to "mama."

It is a nice touch to end the semester with a get-together or a banquet, with the church as a whole or as a separate entity, to reflect on the Lord's goodness. Such a meeting will often take place between Thanksgiving and finals. The students' last week of studies could be enriched by the church providing a care package for the students. Some students will enjoy singing or serving in a Christmas program at the church.

Fall Semester Evaluation Meeting

Once the semester ends, the campus staff worker needs to evaluate the first semester. The campus worker will have three to four weeks before the spring semester begins. This is a good time for him and his family to be refreshed. Campus ministry is extremely draining, and much of campus ministry is late evening work.

SPRING SEMESTER

Annual Basketball Outreach Tournament

An annual basketball tournament can be one of the largest evangelistic pushes of the spring semester. A good goal to pray for is to see eight different student teams sign up to play. Including the players' friends, girlfriends, and the unsaved referees, there might be forty to eighty unsaved people who will hear the gospel challenge at the tournament. Therefore, the campus ministry should have a godly evangelist preach at this event. If the gym facilities are limited, the tournament can be modified to a three-on-three tournament.

Sweetheart Banquet

Depending on the group of students, the campus ministry may want to organize a "sweetheart" banquet around Valentine's Day. Sometimes it would be better to have nothing; other times, it is best to include the dating college couples in the church's sweetheart banquet. Dating is usually one of the hindrances to campus ministry. Often couples are involved in sin which is unpleasant to address, and/or they are so "in love" that they have no time for anyone else including the Lord. College students are often very selfish. The campus life revolves around them and their own little world, and when you add "love" to it, then very little is accomplished for the Lord's sake. Then when they fall "out" of love you normally will lose one if not both from your college-career group because they hate each other or they are so love-sick that they could not stand to see the other dating someone else. The high side of this point is that there will be couples who will do right and the local church will have the privilege to host their wedding. Dates in May and June on the campus ministry need to be left free for such occasions.

Spring College and Career Retreat

The Wilds Christian Camp and Conference Center in Brevard, North Carolina offers a college/career retreat in the fall and spring. The campus ministry may want to encourage students to attend both conferences or stress one. The spring conference is normally close to the students' Spring Break, which can be either very good or very bad for planning purposes. However, by this point in the school year, the campus ministry should have many contacts, as well as a group of students involved in the campus work, who could be encouraged to go to such a retreat. The local church may want to provide sponsors to assist in paying for some of the students who otherwise could not afford to go.

Revivals

The campus ministry needs to take advantage of the church's revival schedule in an assortment of ways. Often the church and campus ministry can coordinate the evangelist's stay with the basketball tournament so the evangelist preaches at the tournament on the Saturday before the meetings start at the church. In addition, the campus ministry should emphasize one night of the revival meetings as a time to encourage many students to attend. Included in this effort may be a pizza party or other fellowship or activity after the service. A dinner on the grounds will also draw students to the services.

The evangelist could also preach on campus in a lecture hall or auditorium or have an open-air meeting. Special permission can be obtained for such outdoor meetings, which are guaranteed to draw a crowd. Special music, testimonies, and preaching are all that is needed.

Spring Break Mission Trip

A mission trip during Spring Break is a tremendous opportunity for outreach for the students. The goal is to prepare an evangelistic opportunity for them on the campus of another college, either one that already has an established campus ministry or one at which a church has a burden to start a campus ministry. Other focuses besides the campus ministry could be targeted for the mission trip, but there is no doubt that the need of the hour is to reach collegians for Christ. As David "served his own generation"[2] and more, so should the students target primarily their own generation.

For a mission trip to be arranged, the two churches involved must communicate early, and the two school Spring Breaks must not

---

[2] Acts 13:36.

coincide. It takes considerable work for both churches, but the results are worth the effort.

The students on the team would need housing and, if possible, some meals provided. It would be good for families in the church to host the students, as this will have a lasting impact on the families regarding the need to reach collegians for Christ. Ideally the students should arrive on Saturday. During the Sunday services, the church should give special emphasis to campus ministry. It would be best if the host church would permit the team to meet with the college/career class and share their burden. It also would be ideal if the Sunday evening service could be dedicated to hearing testimonies from the students and preaching from the campus worker. The students should spend the next three days doing hard pioneer work on the campus. Then the church should allow them some time on Wednesday night to give testimonies from the results of the week. The team then would return home on Thursday, so that the total trip would involve five nights on location. During the trip the campus worker should also meet with the pastor and those who are interested in being involved in the leadership of the campus ministry and give them an overview of campus ministry. The long-term goal is for the host church to start their own campus ministry if they have not already.

One tool that can be used during the team's stay is a sports outreach tournament, such as a three-on-three basketball tournament, which is fitting as Spring Break typically comes in the midst of the hype of the Sweet Sixteen of college basketball.

A more conventional approach is to build to a Tuesday night seminar, ideally to be held on campus, on a topic of interest for students, such as creation vs. evolution. Having the meeting on Tuesday evening will give the group two days on campus to "push" the event. Representatives from the host church should be encouraged to promote and pray for the event in advance and to attend the meeting on campus.

Prior to the mission team's arrival, the host church should arrange to set up a table(s) at a strategic location(s) on campus. Students from the mission team and from the host church and college will "man" the tables, initiating surveys on the topic of the meeting. They will also seek to find students who would be interested in having a Bible study. Members of the local college/career group would follow-up with any interested students, using *The Ploughman's Sower Series*, discussed in chapter eight, which they would be given a "crash course" on to use in an evangelistic Bible study. Tracts and information regarding the host church will also be handed out at the table, and a flier will advertise the special meeting on Tuesday night.

After Tuesday night's message, there will be an invitation to trust Christ and a card for students interested in personal Bible studies to fill out. On Wednesday, visitation teams, ideally made up of one team member and one member of the host church, should immediately follow up with interested students and give the results to the host church for additional follow-up.

At the Wednesday night prayer meeting, team members and people from the host church should have time to give testimonies about the Tuesday night meeting and the various experiences of the week. This testimony time will further fuel the host church's vision of starting a campus ministry. With some measure of effort, the host church could take the fruit of the mission trip and begin the process of chartering a campus ministry for the following school year.

When the mission team returns to its home church, the students should be given an opportunity to give testimony about the Lord's workings. Such testimonies keep the home church steadfast in the burden for campus ministry as well.

The local church should maintain correspondence with the host church and should ask for an evaluation by the host church of the mission team and the week. In addition, the local church should prepare its own evaluation.

The Spring Break mission trip intensifies the need of the students to be on their "spiritual toes" and to be trained in various ways to minister effectively. They receive a greater burden for campus work on their own campus and elsewhere. The trip also increases their burden for lost souls, and the experience may be used to call someone or confirm a call to the full-time ministry of the Word. For the host church, their college and career group will be enthusiastically challenged to start a campus ministry.

There is no need for the host church to provide an offering for the mission team, as the students on the trip are the greatest beneficiaries from the trip. Their faith was increased as they served outside their comfort zones; their unity was enhanced by the gospel camaraderie; their burden for missions was increased; and they are rewarded to know that their Spring Break counted for eternity and was not sown to the flesh!

Graduation Night
The Sunday before finals is the best night to have a graduation testimony service at which all the high school and college graduates are honored. Christian books or Bibles could be presented as gifts, and students could give testimony as to what God has done for them as well as what their future plans are. Several of the college men could preach a short sermon on such an occasion as well. This is a great service to give honor to whom honor is due.

Spring Semester Evaluation Meeting
Same as above for the fall semester evaluation meeting.

SUMMER SEMESTER

May provides an excellent opportunity to evaluate the entire school year and begin planning for the next school year. It also is a good month to have a nationwide student rally or to host a conference for training campus workers.

During the summer, much ministry can be done on the campus, and the campus should not be neglected. Incoming freshmen will attend the summer orientation meeting, and many potential students will be visiting the campus. These occasions give the campus worker an opportunity to meet new students before many of the other campus groups do.

With the need to expand ministries to other campuses being so great, the summer months could also be used for a summer mission trip involving faithful students. They could attach themselves to a good church for the summer and seek to pioneer a campus ministry with that church. One of the best ways for the students to get inside the academic "ivory tower" is to take a class during the summer months for audit or credit. Doing so will put the student missionaries in the mainstream of that campus and will provide many natural contacts and witnessing opportunities. For the campus worker, the summer is a good time to keep in touch with students by letter or e-mail and to work on writing projects, slide presentations, or other projects. For the campus missionary, the summer is prime time to do some needed deputation.

THE CHURCH CALENDAR

There will be special events, services, and activities at the church that the campus worker will coordinate with and integrate into the campus calendar. It does not make sense to schedule an activity with the college students when it would conflict with revival services at the church. Instead the worker can create a night during the revival week that promotes the attendance of college students. Other major services, such as mission conferences, cantatas, or special speakers, should be maximized by the campus worker. Easter is a great time to invite unsaved students to the sunrise service, breakfast, and morning service.

The strength and the breadth of a campus ministry are measured by the students' involvement in the local church and the local church's involvement in the student's life. The church calendar becomes a tremendous tool that the parachurch organization cannot touch. To coordinate the church and campus calendars (and school calendar if the church has a Christian school) is quite a challenge but can be accomplished through regular planning sessions and weekly staff meetings.

STUDENT INVOLVEMENT IN
THE LOCAL CHURCH

The most obvious and perhaps measurable facet of student involvement is the students' attendance at the church services, which is one of the ministry's top goals for the college student. The college student has misplaced priorities if he can attend the fun time on Friday night but sleeps in on Sunday morning. The campus ministry's goal for the student needs to be that he will develop the discipline and the habit of consistently attending the worship services of the church. Aids to this goal have already been suggested with the dinners, lunches, and other activities. The more the families in the church can invite students into their homes and get interested in their lives, the stronger the campus ministry will become. Another aid to attending church services is to provide transportation for those who do not have cars at college. Students can be met at appointed spots on campus or picked up at their residence.

Saved students should be challenged to join the local church while at college. Some churches may have or may want to incorporate a student associate membership. Students who are members will have a much larger assortment of ministries that they can get involved in than the students who are not members. Although there are things that nonmembers can do in most churches, these ministries are limited.

Ministry areas that students can get involved in include

Nursery

Children's ministries

Sunday school

Children's church

Bus ministries

Wednesday night children's programs like Awana, Kids 4 Truth

Vacation Bible School

Children's and youth sports outreach leagues

Youth ministries

Tutoring or mentoring programs for struggling students

Parents' night out (baby-sit for couples)

Nursing home ministries

Ministries for the elderly

Choir or chamber orchestra

Usher crew

Audio/video ministries

Visitation

Maintenance work

Custodial work

Work nights at the church

Missionary prayer breakfasts

Camping and hiking trips

Wedding and baby showers

Church activities should include and involve college students. What a great opportunity the local church has to minister to college students! As the students learn in the environment of the local church, they learn from the godly men and women in the church. The older women can teach the younger women, and the older men can teach the younger men (Titus 2:4). One of the most rewarding aspects of the campus ministry is to see a student get involved in a local church ministry and then graduate and find another church of like faith and get involved in that ministry. It is a blessing to see college students return to visit who are now married, have their own children, and are serving in Bible-believing churches as deacons, Sunday school teachers, youth workers, and even campus workers!

Involvement and participation in the local church is the key to effective discipleship. It is the responsibility of the church staff, deacons, and department heads of the various ministries to be sensitive to the college work force and recruit them for ministry in the church.

The strength of the campus ministry can be measured by how involved the college student is in the local church and how involved the families of the local church are involved in the lives of the students.

11

The Role of the Campus Ministry Mission Board

Up to this point this manual has discussed the history and the present condition of campus ministries. While the scope of campus ministry and the message will not change, the methods might. The greatest need now is to present the need for laborers for the campus. Such laborers will be discussed on several different levels in the next several chapters. Because most churches in a college town are not yet large enough to fully fund a campus pastor, the local church should first approach the campus with a campus missionary, which requires a mission board. Since one of the two greatest omissions in campus ministry has been the lack of the local church's involvement, it would be inconsistent to "press forward" with the need of a mission board divorced from the local churches. Therefore, this chapter will discuss a mission board in connection with the local church.

Vision for a State-Based or Regional Aspect to the Campus Ministry Mission Board

Several approaches could be taken in establishing a campus mission board. In the most localized approach, one local church could handle this responsibility with no outside help or minimal outside accountability. This approach would most likely receive very little support for the overall goals of reaching all secular campuses. The campus mission board could also operate at the state level, based out of a local church with accountability to the supporting pastors of that state or region. This approach has much to commend itself. The other level, beyond a mission board primarily operating at the local and state/regional levels, is for a mission board to operate at the national and international levels. Because most colleges are "state-based" rather than national, it makes the most sense to emphasize the "state-based" or regional aspect in developing a model for campus mission boards. Therefore, this chapter focuses on the national mission board operating at a state or regional level. This places the emphasis where it is needed, the local churches ministering to the local colleges.

Demographic Study of the Colleges in Each State

Every state has its colleges, some more than others, that have students from that state within their student bodies. For example, ninety-two percent of California's high school graduates who attend college attend a college in the state of California. Even in Alaska, the state with the lowest rate of in-state students, forty-two percent of students stay in state for their education.[1] Therefore forty-two to ninety-two percent of any state's college students attend a college within their own state. Typically, the same percentage of these students will remain in the state after graduation.[2] For example, in South Carolina seventy percent of South Carolina's students are amongst the 110,000 students enrolled in the state colleges. After graduation the same percentage of graduates will stay in South Carolina. This statistic is vital for placing the emphasis on each state or region to reach the students in their own state. What fundamental churches need to realize is that enrolled within their state's borders are hometown young men and women that need the gospel. If churches did not reach these young people prior to going to college, they will find them funneled into a few colleges within each state. This will be the most strategic place and time to reach the future leaders of each state. Reaching them while at college is much easier than reaching them after they graduate. The Lord has permitted students to be corralled for four years in churches' very back yards

---

[1]The Ivy Jungle Network, "The Campus Ministry Update," November 2000.
[2]Ibid.

so that those churches can concentrate their evangelistic efforts on the students.

Sadly, many churches do not share a vision for campus work, especially if the campus missionary is basing his work out of state or out of the region. It is difficult for them to support such a work, especially if they do not see that the campuses are a tremendous mission field with international potential. However, if a campus ministry begins with a statewide or regional focus, stressing the fivefold scope of ministry and the fact that many of the graduates will end up in the state, there is greater hope that the churches within the state will shoulder this burden. Therefore, the goal of the state-level or regional aspect of the mission board is to inform, educate, and promote the need of all the fundamental churches within the state or region to pray for and to fund the needed campus ministries of their state's or regional colleges.

Strategy to Target First the Larger Colleges in Each State

How does this vision get off the ground for each state? The best approach is to have a model to follow that each state can replicate, modify, and use for its own needs. Keep in mind it is possible to have so much string on the organizational kite that the campus ministry never has a chance to get off the ground. The first step in establishing the state-wide or regional vision and aspect of the campus mission board is to study the state/region and the demographics of its colleges. A list of every college and university and their student enrollment figures should be created. Based on those numbers, the regional or state-wide coordinator of the mission board should place the colleges into the following categories:

NUMBER OF STUDENTS	CATEGORY
0–4,999 students	Small colleges
5,000–9,999 students	Medium colleges
10,000–19,999 students	Large colleges
20,000+	Extra-large colleges

After completing this, the coordinator or his delegate(s) should locate every college on a state map. The extra-large, large, and the medium colleges should then be especially highlighted. It is no accident that every city in which the apostle Paul planted a church was a major college town and that the most fruitful of all Paul's church-planting efforts was the church in Ephesus, which he based originally on a college campus, the Hall of Tyrannus. Therefore, as one looks at the map, there will be certain "hot spots" that are key college towns. These larger campuses should be given higher priority in planting churches and starting campus ministries. The statewide/regional coordinator/representative should survey established churches in these towns and assist those with the aptitude to start a campus ministry. Towns with large colleges that have no fundamental works should be targeted by the state as key sites for church-planting projects. Using South Carolina as an example, there is only one college that has over 20,000 students (University of South Carolina), two colleges with 10,000 to 19,999 students (Clemson University and College of Charleston/The Citadel), and two with enrollment between 5,000 and 9,999 (Winthrop University and Bob Jones University).

In addition, if there are several colleges in an adjoining area that have a combined student population of more than 5000 students, these schools should be highlighted as well (e.g., in Spartanburg, South Carolina, there are several colleges that meet this criterion). After completing the study, the coordinator should prioritize which campuses within the state or region should be targeted to place missionaries. This listing will also be affected by the local church in the college town, as the home church must be burdened for such a ministry and have the suitable aptitude for reaching college students. Sometimes the smaller colleges in a state will be targeted first because there are good churches ready to begin a campus ministry in these towns. Once a campus ministry is established on a larger campus, manpower can be produced to start other campus ministries at smaller neighboring colleges. It is not uncommon for a campus missionary to work several campuses; nor should it be uncommon for churches and mission boards to think in these expanding terms. The long-term goal for the mission board is to have a gospel witness on each of the larger campuses in each of our fifty states.

Dividing the State into Zones for Pastors' Meetings

After prioritizing ministries, the coordinator should divide the state into regions. This could be done by observing the natural divisions; such as counties, hunting regions, or political units. For example, South Carolina is nicely divided into three regions: the high country (upstate), the midlands, and the low country. After these divisions are made, the regional coordinator should identify the major colleges and the fundamental churches in these zones. Then the coordinator and the pastors involved in campus ministry should host luncheons for other pastors, their staffs, and their missionary committee. These luncheons will be held in each of the zones. At these luncheons the coordinator or his delegate should present the vision for reaching collegians for Christ within the state. Testimonies, reports, slide presentations, and other materials can be used to maximize the ninety-minute luncheon. At the meeting the pastors should be given the opportunity to ask questions about the campus ministry and to sign up to host a campus missionary and his team for a deputation meeting. These meetings can be used to identify future members for the mission board's advisory board, pastors in the college town who want to begin a campus ministry, and pastors who want to assist the statewide/regional project of reaching the secular campuses with the gospel.

As outlined so far, the process for establishing the regional aspect of the campus ministry mission board must be initiated by someone within the state/region. This is the model that has been followed in West Virginia and South Carolina. Within each state, pastors need to get burdened for campus work and take the initiative to push forward with their statewide/regional goals. However, in most cases a campus ministry will start with one pastor in a college town seeing the need of having a campus missionary. Each state/region will need initially one base and one pastor to get the "ball rolling." This pastor must be doctrinally sound and practically blameless, a man of vision, and a man willing to extend himself beyond the fifteen-mile radius of his own church. Then a handful of pastors in the state/region need to be given the vision and rally around the cause of reaching collegians for Christ in their region. The goal should be to have at least one training hub in each region where pastors and their workers can be trained and equipped to start and maintain their own campus ministries.

It is important to keep in mind that the campus ministry is to be based out of the local church and that the campus workers are primarily accountable to their local churches. It is also important to recognize that although most full-time campus workers will be initially funded as missionaries, the long-term goal is for the larger local churches to fully absorb the campus missionary into the office of campus pastor. As this goal is realized, his missionary monies can be released to assist other campus missionaries and their projects. The goal is for the missionary to work himself out of missionary support and to be fully funded by the local church where he serves. This example would follow the church-planting model, where the church planter's goal is to grow the ministry so that he no longer needs outside support but that the ministry becomes self-supporting. The goal is not to have campus workers indefinitely or permanently supported by missionary funds, but for campus missionaries to see their local church grow by their labors where they can be fully supported. It is imperative that the mission board and churches have the goal of having a full-time campus pastor to serve on staff of the church that neighbors a large campus. At first the campus worker may need missionary support, but this is ideally only a short-term goal and need.

The Campus Pastor/Missionary's Loyalties
It must be clearly communicated to all parties that the campus pastor/missionary is responsible first to the Lord, then to the local church he is ministering in, and then to the mission board and his supporting churches. Historically, the loyalties for campus ministries have been either

> The missionary to his/her mission board first; no loyalty to local church (the parachurch model) or
>
> The missionary to his/her mission board first; then secondly, loyalty to the local church (the missionary model).

These two models are unsatisfactory, as there must be loyalty to the local church. The second model works and is a step in the right direction, but it can become very complicated if the two heads giving direction to the campus work are not in agreement. Also, under this model the local church can lose its entire campus ministry overnight if the missionary relocates his church base across town. Therefore, the closer the campus missionary is tied to the local church, the better. The campus missionary/pastor needs to be seen as an insider on staff, integrally involved in the ministry and knit to the organizational framework of the church. The best approach when a church does not have the resources to hire a campus pastor is to approach campus ministry in the same manner as a church-planting project. However, such an approach for campus ministry has never been presented. It has happened at times by default or through a church split, but there has never been a deliberate structure where the fundamentalist did it on purpose. Such a structure for a mission board is presented in the remainder of this chapter, using Cross Impact Ministries (formerly Spurgeon Foundation Campus Ministries) as an example.

VISION OF CROSS IMPACT MINISTRIES' ORGANIZATIONAL STRUCTURE

Jesus Christ "the head of the body, the church" (Col. 1:18)

President of Cross Impact Ministries

Director of Mission Board

Executive Board Members—President, Director, Regional Directors, Pastors, etc.

Regional Coordinators (8)—Pastors with a campus ministry in the state

Advisory Board Members—Pastors, Evangelists, Missionaries, Educators, etc.

Financial Committee (4)—Treasurer, Assistant Treasurer, two board members

Secretary—Member of Executive Board

Home Office—secretary, office workers

Cross Impact Press

Campus Evangelists

Cross Impact Missionaries—covered in chapter thirteen

The Executive Board

The president of the executive board provides the general leadership and oversight of the campus ministry, chairing all meetings of the executive board. The executive board would include the director of the mission board, regional directors and Christian workers who have a unique burden for campus ministry. They are accountable to one another for maintaining doctrinal purity and godly ministry. The executive board will interview and approve all missionary candidates, hire and terminate Cross Impact Ministries' employees as necessary, and assist in handling staff and missionary problems.

Advisory Board

The advisory board consists of pastors within the various states or regions that share the same doctrine, ministry integrity, and goal of reaching collegians for Christ. Their role is to meet at the regional advisory board meetings, the annual board meeting at the annual campus conference, and to give counsel and support to the campus ministry goals. This group provides an additional level of accountability and reinforces the need to "hold fast"[3] to sound doctrine and practices. The goal of Cross Impact Ministries is to have a nationwide presence, dividing the country into eight regions.

The advisory board can recommend missionary candidates to the executive board and can assist in the interview process. They provide the core support to the organization by praying for the ministry of campus work and sacrificially funding the needs of the pioneer works. They can challenge their businessmen to invest in the campus ministry. They also assist in promoting the campus ministry by informing students from their churches of the ministry and by recruiting campus missionaries. These pastors can also host luncheons for pastors interested in campus ministry, which is a tremendous help to the cause of campus work. They can serve as guest speakers at various campus outings, conferences, rallies, revivals, retreats, or other activities and can write materials for the campus ministry. They can bring their own college/career group to join in the various outreaches and fellowships of the campus ministry. The advisors

---

[3]2 Tim. 1:13.

can also serve as recruiters for the campus ministry at various Bible colleges, fellowships, and missionary conferences. In addition, they can be part of the faculty at the annual training base for campus workers and can promote adding training for campus ministry to the curriculum at Bible colleges.

The Financial Committee
The financial committee includes a treasurer, an assistant treasurer, and two members of the executive board. The committee is responsible for receipting all giving to the campus ministry and for spending approval, which will follow the executive board's guidelines. In addition, members of the financial committee present the financial records at the advisory board meetings. These records should be audited annually by an outside agency. The financial committee may also be responsible for overseeing group health insurance for the missionaries if the local churches do not have insurance policies.

Campus Ministry Secretary
The campus ministry secretary is a member of the executive board and is responsible for chronicling the process of the campus ministry. The secretary takes minutes of all executive board meetings and keeps a record of all minutes, agendas, and other information. Campus ministry secretaries are needed also at the regional level and are selected from the advisory board members of that region.

Home Office for the Campus Ministry
The office personnel of the home office will perform all necessary office tasks, such as correspondence, receptionist work, filing financial records, and receipting donors. The home office absorbs the expense for personnel, postage, phone, and other related items.

The southeast regional hub of Cross Impact Ministries is housed at University Baptist Church (UBC) in Clemson, South Carolina. The northeast hub is located in Williston, VT at Trinity Baptist Church. The Rocky Mountain zone hub is found in Westminster, Colorado at Tri-City Baptist Church.

The southeast zone (five states) would include Florida, Georgia, South Carolina, North Carolina and Tennessee. The mid-Atlantic zone (six states) would include Delaware, New Jersey, Maryland, Pennsylvania, Virginia and West Virginia. The New England zone (seven states) would include Maine, New Hampshire, Vermont, Massachusetts, Rhode Island, Connecticut and New York. The mid-eastern zone (six states) would include Michigan, Ohio, Kentucky, Indiana, Illinois and Wisconsin. The south-central zone (six states) would include Alabama, Mississippi, Arkansas, Louisiana, Oklahoma and Texas. The mid-central zone (seven states) would include Kansas, Missouri, Nebraska, Iowa, North Dakota, South Dakota and Minnesota. The mountain zone (seven states) would include Montana, Idaho, Wyoming, Utah, Colorado, New Mexico and Arizona. The Pacific zone (six states) would include Washington, Oregon, Nevada, California, Alaska and Hawaii.

Cross Impact Press
Cross Impact Press is the publishing arm of Cross Impact Ministries and is responsible for the printing of the campus ministry's newsletters, promotional materials, brochures, artwork, slide presentations, discipleship materials, books, tracts, letterheads, envelopes, and other printed materials.

The Director of Cross Impact Ministries
The director of the campus ministry is a member of the executive board who represents the campus ministry at the national level. He promotes the campus ministry at missionary fairs at the various fundamental, separated Bible colleges and Christian universities. He assists in the interviewing and recruiting of missionary candidates, recommends the candidates to the executive board, and assists in placing the missionaries. In addition, the director attends all executive board meetings related to the campus ministry and participates in the training of the campus missionary. He also assists the campus missionaries in their deputation, mission trips, and retreats. The director should also contribute to the writing ministries of the campus ministry and assist in surveying and pioneering new campus mission fields. In addition, the director handles any necessary confrontations with missionaries and/or pastors and handles any board problems and relationships with other churches and missionaries.

Director of International Ministries

The director of international ministries is also a member of the executive board and directs the overseas ministries of Cross Impact Ministries. He promotes the foreign missions aspect of Cross Impact Ministries and represents Cross Impact Ministries at mission's conferences. The director also assists missionaries during deputation and assists student mission teams. He interviews any potential foreign missionaries, and he participates in the preaching and teaching at the annual Cross Impact Ministries' campus conference and candidate school and attends all executive board and advisory board meetings.

Campus Evangelist

The campus evangelist is a member of the executive board and assists the campus ministries in personal evangelism. He trains campus pastors in soulwinning and evangelistic approaches for reaching students on the secular campuses. He also preaches at campus meetings, outdoor revivals, tournaments, and other events. The campus evangelist develops attractive soulwinning tracts, literature, and other materials geared for collegians. In addition, he assists in promoting the campus ministry at meetings and other churches and assists in training missionary candidates at the Cross Impact Ministries' candidate school. He preaches and assists with the different student mission teams on deputation and on their appointed mission field.

Advisory Board Meetings

To involve the advisory board, the mission board should schedule at least three meetings a year, perhaps around social functions of the campus ministry. For example, it would not be difficult to schedule an advisory board meeting during the fall semester on the weekend of a home football game. On such a weekend, the host church and campus ministry could organize a "Rally in the Valley" (a fall semester kick-off retreat scheduled around the first home football game) or a college/career conference in which the various pastors of the advisory board preach to the students. Not only would their preaching be a great blessing to the students, but also the pastors would gain a greater burden and vision for campus ministry and the spiritual needs of the students. During the spring semester, a meeting could be scheduled during a college basketball game; and at the end of the spring semester and near the beginning of the summer sessions, an advisory board meeting could be scheduled around a college baseball game. The advisory board meetings can also be scheduled at different church and campus locations during the year to further spread the burden of campus work throughout the state. It would be good, for instance, to rotate meetings through the various regions or zones of the state so that pastors throughout the state are able to attend. Pastors not on the advisory board should also be invited to attend these meetings because this is a statewide/regional ministry that should be shouldered by the churches in the state or region.

At the advisory meetings the staff and deacons of the host church should spend time greeting each of the pastors and their friends and handing out an agenda for the meeting. This agenda should include the dates, times, and location of the next advisory board meeting. During the meeting a short challenge should be given by one of the pastors, and students should give testimonies about what God is doing in their lives on the campus. In addition to their testimonies, the various campus workers should give an overview of the previous semester and the goals for the new semester. This information should be communicated orally and in writing. In addition, the minutes of the previous meeting need to be approved, and the financial committee should present a financial report and some of the financial goals and needs of the ministry. Any old business should be reviewed and any new business presented. The presiding pastor should give a time for discussion and questions and answers. If need be, the group could discuss any key issues that the campus work is facing. Campus projects need to be presented and volunteers enlisted. Recommendations for campus workers should be made at these meetings as well. The host church should also plan a dinner or a luncheon and allot time for fellowship. For portions of these luncheons, the pastors' wives and families could attend, and a special activity could be planned for the ladies and children when the business and details of the campus ministry need to be discussed. After the meeting the office staff should promptly mail the minutes of the meeting to each pastor in attendance and pastors interested in the campus ministry.

The Role of the Churches within the State or Region

The idea must be communicated to the pastors in the state that this is a state or regional project and needs their prayerful and financial support. This statewide/regional vision is important for many reasons. First, the campus ministry needs much prayer support. Second, campus ministry is very expensive and needs financial support.

In addition to prayer and financial support, there are other ways local churches can get involved in the statewide/regional goal of reaching collegians, such as hosting a meeting with the campus worker and the students to allow them to present the vision for campus ministry. These meetings keep the goal before the churches and create further networking for student contacts on the campuses, as the campus worker will ask at each meeting if there are any students at the college that the campus ministry could visit. In addition, by visiting other churches, the young college converts see that there are other churches of like precious faith as their home church. Such visits also assist in recommending students to churches within the state after they graduate, especially if they have already visited the church and have a favorable impression.

In addition, some churches may have the perfect facilities or camps to host college/career/campus meetings or host an international retreat. The church could also participate in the annual Cross Impact Campus Ministry Conference or enter teams in the various sports outreaches. These sports outreaches could be held with a statewide competition at which the gospel would be preached. Such outreaches could be a great evangelism tool for the college/career groups of the state.

The Lasting Benefits of Involvement

The statewide/regional luncheons and meetings provide fellowship among the various pastors, their wives, and their churches. They give to the churches in the state/region a statewide/regional goal that can be shared. The network of churches is healthy and godly and will provide many good contacts. As it relates to the campus ministry, this network will provide contacts of students going to college and then in turn will recommend students back to the churches. The churches in the state will indirectly benefit by campus ministry and, in many cases, will directly benefit with students being funneled to their church. The entire state will benefit by fundamental campus ministry as the state sees its future leaders influenced by the gospel of Jesus Christ. The long-term dividends will be rich for the Bible colleges and seminaries, as they reap in the men and women called into the full-time ministry of the Word of God. Local churches can invite the international students to their churches and mission conferences and literally have the world attend their annual conferences. The campus ministry will challenge pastors of local churches to give more attention to their own college/career group's needs. Christian camps, in due time, will see an increase at their college/career retreats. There is an innumerable amount of blessings that flow out of the fundamental churches' efforts to have a statewide campus outreach through a joint missionary effort.

12

The Vision for America's Campuses: The Pastoral Manager of the Campus Ministry

One of the most neglected mission fields in America is the secular college campus. The world's future leaders are training at these colleges. There are not too many places in the world where one could find such a conglomeration of the cream of the crop. On the campus in Clemson, there are more than seventy nations represented. Indeed, the world is in America's backyard. The cults and the new evangelicals have feasted on such a harvest field, where young men and women crystallize their worldview, secure their religious convictions, choose their vocation, and often find their spouse. Sadly, the fundamentalist has abandoned the secular campus. Today, if one surveys the landscape of secular college campuses, he will find no more than fifty campuses that have any fundamentalist influence. Of those fifty or fewer ministries, most are struggling to establish a core group of students to actually do the work of the ministry on the campus. The need of the hour is for pastors to see the need to establish fundamental campus ministries that are local-church-based. To get the big picture, the pastor/manager in a college town should have in view four goals relating to campus ministry:

Goal #1   To present the gospel of Jesus Christ *locally*, to one's neighboring secular college (For example, UBC's goal is to reach the more than 18,000 college students at Clemson University.)

Goal #2   To present the gospel of Jesus Christ *statewide* (For example, UBC's goal statewide is to reach the more than 110,000 college students in the state of South Carolina.)

Goal #3   To create a model for reaching collegians *nationwide* (For example, UBC's goal is for South Carolina to be a model that could be replicated in all 50 states.)

     A. To present the gospel to the 15 million college students in America

     B. To present the gospel to the more than 600,000 international students in America

Goal #4   To promote evangelism/church planting and campus ministries *worldwide* in the college towns of other nations

This manual focuses primarily on goals two and three. This focus is not to suggest that UBC has achieved goal number one to the Lord's satisfaction but that it is at the point that the burden for campus ministry must be multiplied and that the fundamentalist movement must be striving together to reach these goals. The challenge of managing these goals at local, state/regional, national, and worldwide levels is overwhelming, but it is not out of the reach of God's grace. These goals are laced with managerial nightmares. Some of these problems will be addressed idealistically and then relegated to the realm of cold reality.

The managerial burden for the campus ministry must rest on the pastor in a college town. He needs to have a burden for reaching collegians for Christ. This burden must be conveyed to his church family and proper emphasis given to the fact that the secular campus is a needy mission field. It is justifiable to seek a missionary to minister full-time on America's larger secular campuses. It cannot be emphasized enough that the secular campus is a mission field and that the local church in a college town does not have the option to overlook it, unless it wants to disobey the Great Commission. If God has providentially placed His church near a college campus, it is safe to say that He desires that church to have a campus ministry.

THE PROBLEM OF TOO FEW WORKERS

The first problem for the pastor/manager with such goals is the need of workers to labor on the secular campus. How can the lost hear the good news that Jesus saves without a preacher, a Christian worker/witness? There are few being called to campus ministry because there are few aware of the needs of the secular campus. The pastor/manager must not only present this vision to his own church in a college town, but the vision must mount up with wings and be presented to other pastors, churches, Bible colleges, etc. Without fundamentalists having the vision for reaching collegians for Christ, students will perish, and Christians will miss one of the greatest opportunities to win the next generation of leaders to Christ.

THE PROBLEM OF INADEQUATELY TRAINED WORKERS

The spiritual and academic qualifications of campus workers should be defined early. First Timothy 3 and Titus 1 serve as the best description of what is needed for the campus worker, but with the unique ministry of ministering to those in "Athens," other considerations need to be sorted through. One question is how much formal training is required for the campus worker? Obviously, God is not limited to using only people with a bachelor's or master's degree to minister on a secular campus; however; the people on a college campus do have a high appreciation for education. Because of the fivefold scope of campus ministry, the ideal campus worker has a PhD, is married, and speaks English, Chinese, French, German, and Spanish fluently. Realistically, the worker should have at least an undergraduate degree and should plan to complete a graduate program in order to understand the needs of the graduate student. My recommendation is that the college worker have an undergraduate degree and a graduate Bible degree. The master of divinity is ideal for the campus worker. Such a high academic standard may limit at first the number of eligible campus workers, but the campus ministry is not a typical ministry.

Very few churches or Bible colleges include training for campus workers, a fact that exposes the second problem for the pastor/manager of campus ministries to overcome: the problem of specific training for the secular campus. There are four ways that such training can be received. First, training could be received in a formal setting, such as at the Bible college. This would necessitate that the Bible college include training for the campus ministry in its curriculum. Although most Bible colleges include curriculum about the ministries of children, youth, the Christian family, missions, church planting, possibly even nursing homes, no colleges have consistently included the campus ministry in their curriculum. Such an addition would give the needed exposure to this neglected ministry and would multiply efforts in having men prepared to minister on the secular campus.

A second form of training is for local churches to recruit extension workers from fundamental Bible colleges to assist in the church's ministry to the secular campus. These extension workers would be required to take the class on campus ministry and/or special training from the workers of the local church before being "turned loose" on the secular campus. Such training is necessary because many students who have not been exposed to public education at any level need additional training to understand the culture and mindset of the secular student. Often, without such training, the well-intentioned believer will ignorantly repel the unsaved student and make it more difficult for the local church to reach him for Christ. Such problems particularly arise with international students. For example, a Chinese student will easily pray with the extension worker "to be saved" to please the worker but typically will have had no genuine conversion experience. The extension worker's zeal must be tempered with knowledge that is procured through training. Because the extension workers must be mature to reach their peers on the secular campus, upperclassmen and graduate students are generally more suited for this type of extension work. For Bible college students interested in campus ministry, the extension ministry presents them with the opportunity to experientially explore God's will as to future service that may include campus ministry. It is a win-win situation for the student and the local church.

A third training method is for the interested preacher to intern with a local church that has a thorough outreach to its secular campus. The internship could last from one summer, to a semester, to a year. This type of hands-on training would be invaluable, especially if the intern is planning to go to another local church and pioneer a campus ministry. The fourth means of training is for the campus worker to attend conferences/seminars on the topic of the campus ministry.

At present, opportunities for training using all of these means are available. For example, Bob Jones University and Northland Baptist Bible College have added this dimension to their ministerial training. Bob Jones University will be offering a class on reaching the secular campus via their LINC classes. Northland offers the class as a block class elective. In addition, extension workers from Bob Jones University are being informally trained through Cross Impact Ministries in Clemson, South Carolina, and internships are being offered through Cross Impact Ministries at University Baptist Church. Every year, Cross Impact Ministries sponsors a conference (Cross Impact Campus Ministries Conference) for campus workers and those interested in starting campus ministries. Some strides are being made in training opportunities, but more will be needed to properly train the campus pastor/missionary.

THE PROBLEM OF FUNDING A CAMPUS PASTOR

A third problem that the pastor/manager faces is the inability of most local churches in a college town to fund a full-time campus pastor. As previously discussed, the pastor/manager has four options for staffing this outreach. The pastor or another existing staff worker can add this ministry to his responsibilities. However, the pastor and his staff are typically already on overload and consequently are very limited as to how much time they can spend on the campus, a fact that significantly decreases the effectiveness of the campus ministry. Another approach is to organize the college/career Sunday school class to minister to the campus with the Sunday school teacher as the director. This can be done, but again the limitations are minimal campus time for the worker and often the lack of students to form a core group to do the work of the ministry. Until a core group of saved students attending the secular college is created, there will be little campus ministry accomplished. The third option is to seek a campus missionary who will work out of the local church. This is a healthy option but is not without challenges, which will be discussed later in this chapter. The ultimate goal, option number four, is to have a full-time campus pastor.

It would be wonderful if every local church in a college town could hire a full-time campus pastor who has been formally trained in campus ministries, has benefited by campus extension work, and has been thoroughly trained with hands-on experience through a one-year campus internship. However, the reality is that most college-town churches cannot immediately fund such a position. Where then does the pastor/manager start, especially if the church's budget cannot fund another full-time staff worker?

The best starting point is for the pastor himself to get involved in the process of ministering to college students. If possible, the pastor, his staff, and/or his lay leadership should attend one of the Cross Impact Ministries conferences that instruct the local church on all the "nuts and bolts" of starting, maintaining, and expanding a campus ministry. This conference equips the church to take the quantum leaps to get on campus to have a Bible study. Although the pastor's time is very limited, the exposure and time spent on the campus will increase his burden for the secular campus. His schedule may allow only one block of time during the week to visit or to conduct a Bible study on the campus, but it will be invaluable for shaping his philosophy of ministry to the secular campus and for experientially teaching him what subsequent workers will face. The pastor must take the lead in this ministry and then begin to delegate the hands-on outreach to someone else. The most logical next step is to consider the leadership of the college/career Sunday school, which should have been included from the very beginning of the process to reach collegians. Much of the campus ministry could be organized through this Sunday school class. Again, it will not be too long before the Sunday school class will feel frustrated with their inability to give the campus the attention that it really needs. This holy frustration will be used to fuel the vision of getting a campus missionary to assist in reaching collegians for Christ.

To find a campus missionary, the local church can contact Cross Impact Ministries, which works with solid, fundamental churches to place campus missionaries. Unlike parachurch campus ministries, Cross Impact Ministries recognizes the place of the local church as God's divine instrument of ministry for this age and clearly presents that the missionary's loyalty is to the Lord first and then to his local church. Cross Impact Ministries seeks to make it clear that the campus missionary is first the church's staff worker and second a Cross Impact Ministries missionary. This parallels the practice of indigenous church-planting principles. The goal is ultimately for that church to grow to the point that their campus worker is completely supported by the church's budget. When this takes place, the local church has in place what is the most effective staffing for reaching a college campus: a college pastor.

Cross Impact Ministries seeks to assist local churches in any of the leadership phases just listed. Cross Impact Ministries seeks to work only with separated, fundamental churches that are baptistic in nature, including fundamental Bible churches and independent Baptist churches. These churches should have a healthy balance between evangelism and discipleship and should not be running down any theological "rabbit trails," such as the KJV-only issue and five-point Calvinism. It is also important that the local church stress holiness and high music standards, as secular college students will especially need training in these areas. Cross Impact Ministries provides services ranging from simple consultation for the local church that wants to establish a campus ministry, to training of church staff or lay leadership, to discipleship materials, to assistance in match-making a campus missionary to the local church. Churches interested in having their own campus missionary must submit an application to Cross Impact Ministries. This application includes the church's doctrinal statement, philosophy for ministry, ministry associations, proximity to the secular campus, and aptitude of the church for campus ministry. The application is followed up with an interview between the local pastor and Cross Impact Ministries. If the local church and Cross Impact Ministries are doctrinally and philosophically compatible, the process begins to match a missionary with that local church or to train their recommended worker for the campus ministry.

Once approval has been given by Cross Impact Ministries for a campus missionary, the pastor of the local church needs to further prepare his church family for this additional dimension to their ministry. The missionary will need the support of not only the pastor but also the church family. The true strength of a college ministry is measured by the involvement level of the students in the ministries of the local church and, conversely, the involvement of the church family in the lives of the students. One very tangible way of showing support is through the prayer and financial support of the church. The campus pastor/missionary needs to be viewed not only as a missionary to the campus but also as a church staff worker. It is strongly recommended that the campus pastor/missionary have an office in the local church and be included in all staff meetings, deacons meetings, and similar events. The more he can be integrated into the mainstream of the church, the more effective his ministry will be. Again, the long-term goal is to fully absorb the missionary financially into the church's budget and to recognize him as a full-time pastor and employee of the church. Also, it cannot be emphasized enough that the goal of the campus ministry is to see students saved, baptized, added to the local church, discipled, and involved in some aspect of the ministry of the local church. Most campus ministries divorce themselves from the local church. Consequently when their members graduate they often do not get involved in a local church because that was not part of their training.

The Problem of Lack of Involvement by the Senior Pastor

The third problem dealt with the inability of the local church funding the position for a college pastor. The solution is for the church to consider a campus pastor/missionary, which leads to a fourth problem for the pastor/manager of the campus ministry: helping to secure the proper support and funding for his campus pastor/missionary. Emphasis is placed on the pastor/manager doing all he can to assist the campus pastor/missionary in raising the necessary support. This is especially needed because the campus pastor/missionary will have his work cut out for him to raise support for a home missions project on a very misunderstood mission field. One obstacle the missionary will need to overcome is the warped and shortsighted view that home missions is not really missions. As previously emphasized, if any ministry is world missions, it is the campus ministry. The potential for efficiently reaching the world is evident by the 600,000 international students who will be the world's leadership.

Another obstacle for the missionary is the difficulty some churches have to see the need to reach collegians for Christ. Some rural churches will have little regard for education or will feel intimidated by the entire concept of a campus ministry. Some pastors will have little burden or vision for assisting some local church reach the mission field in their backyard and to provide funds for "their staff." Some pastors are misinformed regarding the compromising ministries such as Campus Crusade, InterVarsity, and Navigators and will ask the question, "Why do we need to reinvent the wheel when we have such fine groups already doing the job?" These obstacles will be addressed and a strategy presented later in this chapter, but no doubt the missionary has an uphill battle to gain his support. However, this mountain can be brought down if the pastor/manager of a campus ministry does what he can to assist the missionary in raising support. For example, the pastor can assist his campus pastor/missionary by

1. Presenting the burden, vision and long-term goals for absorbing the campus pastor/missionary into the church's budget. This would include a plan to increase his salary each year. It is critical for the deacons and the church to know the direction for this office and to support it.

2. Seeking housing for the missionary couple from within the church family or providing them with a parsonage if one is available.

3. Initiating a food pounding when the missionary comes. An installment service would be appropriate at the arrival of the campus missionary and a possible offering taken for the new workers.

4. Hosting a pastor's luncheon to introduce the campus missionary to other pastors and to encourage scheduling the couple for a deputation meeting and especially considering them for mission conferences.

5. Writing a form letter to be used in a mail-out to other pastors.

The bottom line is that the pastor and the church family must be sensitive to the needs of the campus pastor/missionary. Cross Impact Ministries' vision is for the local church to take on more of the financial responsibility for its campus pastor/missionary each year. The support level for the missionary is established by the local church and Cross Impact Ministries. Cross Impact Ministries suggests that the local church support the missionary at a minimum of twenty-five percent of that level for the first year and have in place a plan that will absorb all financial responsibilities within a seven-year period, such as in the following example.

1. The local church and mission board set a goal: example of $36,000 a year ($3,000 a month).

2. The local church must start by supporting the missionary at twenty-five percent ($750 a month).

3. The local church sets, at a maximum, a seven-year goal to fully support the missionary. This goal requires a $375 increase per year. This figure does not include needed cost-of-living increases.

Year	Local Church Support	Outside Missionary Support
1	$750 a month	$2250
2	$1125 a month (increase by $375 a month)	$1875
3	$1500 a month (increase by $375 a month)	$1500
4	$1875 a month (increase by $375 a month)	$1125
5	$2250 a month (increase by $375 a month)	$750
6	$2625 a month (increase by $375 a month)	$375
7	$3000 a month (increase by $375 a month)	$0

Some churches will be able to absorb the campus pastor/missionary in less than seven years, while other churches may need more time for church growth to catch up with the extra staff needs. The key is progress and keeping the goal before the deacons and church family. Annual reviews and evaluations should take place between the pastor and his campus pastor/missionary. There should also be an annual review between the pastor, missionary, and Cross Impact Ministries to review progress and to address any concerns. There needs to be a measure of accountability at each of these points. As the need of missionary support diminishes, those funds can recycle into the Cross Impact Ministries and can be used for other local churches seeking to have a campus pastor/missionary. In due time,

God willing, Cross Impact Ministries would have the resources to quickly accelerate the deputation process for the missionary.

The Problem of Maintaining the Many Relationships

The fifth problem that the pastor/manager may face in the campus ministry is maintaining the many relationships when a church has a campus pastor/missionary. The first relationship that must be maintained is between him and his campus pastor/missionary. He needs to treat the campus worker as he would any other church staff worker and needs to keep open lines of communication with this worker. He must set the direction for the work that he wants to see accomplished on the campus as well as how he wants to involve the campus worker and the students in the local church. He must clearly present his expectations for his campus worker as to how many hours he expects him to work on campus and in the office each week. At a minimum, the campus worker should spend fifteen hours a week on the campus, with a good goal being twenty hours. Imagine what would happen if pastors spent fifteen to twenty hours a week on the type of visitation that emphasizes evangelism and personal discipleship! The pastor should also give opportunities for the campus worker to preach in his pulpit and to keep the church informed about the needs of his ministry. The pastor must reinforce, from the pulpit, the work on the campus and the need for the church family to get involved in the lives of the students who will start attending the church. He also needs to inform the church, especially a church that has had little exposure to college students, that at first many of the students may dress immodestly or wear earrings from their ears to their navels to their toes. Some of the students may bring to church a sorry paraphrased Bible or a Catholic Bible. It is important that the church family receive them graciously and work with them patiently. College students who get saved and are given well-presented scriptural reasons for standards in such areas as music and dress will generally respond favorably and grow quickly. However, if someone drops a judgmental hammer on them, they will pull the Houdini act on church. Most college students are biblically illiterate; it takes time to lay a scriptural foundation. It is also important for the pastor and local church to realize that many of the students that the campus missionary works with will never enter their church. With some students, it takes time just to get them to come to church. Also, many students go home on weekends. It is important to keep in mind that God's Word will not return void and that many of the college contacts will get saved later and will begin attending church then. For example, UBC has had students call years later to tell the church that they were saved in one of the Bible studies and that they are now involved in a good fundamental church or have been called into the ministry. Campus work is slow going at first, but once an undergraduate core group is formed, it will take off! A church should not put undue pressure on its campus worker for immediate numbers and new faces in church. They will come, but the church must be patient and be an encouragement to the campus worker.

The pastor must also consider the relationship between his church and the churches supporting the campus missionary, particularly when he is defining the campus missionary's job description. Because at first other churches are supporting the missionary to do campus work, it is only right for the worker to be on that campus and to spend the majority of his time in work that deals with college students. A good rule of thumb is for the campus pastor/missionary to spend the same percentage of his time in direct campus work as the percentage of outside support he receives. For example, if the church is supporting the campus pastor/missionary for twenty-five percent of his support, the pastor could ethically and properly assign twenty-five percent of the campus pastor/missionary's time to ministries not related to the campus. The pastor/manager does not want to give the impression to supporting churches that he is misappropriating their funds.

This introduces another responsibility that the pastor/manager needs to maintain: the spirit of appreciation for the churches supporting his campus worker. Periodic notes of thanks would go a long way in expressing this appreciation to these churches. He may also want to host such pastors to thank them for their support and may want to consider taking them to one of the sporting events of the college. Another way of involving these supporting pastors is for the campus missionary to arrange for his supporting pastors to speak to the students on the campus. Also, the pastor/manager must realize that those same churches would like to see their missionary from time to time to receive updates of the campus ministry. This means that the pastor must be sensitive to his campus worker's making such visits and being away from the local church periodically. Such absences will also be necessary if the missionary needs to raise some additional support. He also needs to make sure that his campus worker is communicating regularly with his supporting churches. Those supporting churches in the state need to keep the perspective that the large college campus is a mission field. The best way to fund the campus missionary is for the financial burden to rest upon the churches within each state. The secular campuses within each state should be a targeted ministry for all the fundamental churches to cooperate in reaching. A healthy campus ministry will ultimately benefit the entire state and its churches. Some of the finest pastors, evangelists, and missionaries were saved on secular campuses. The question is often raised, "Where is the next generation of missionaries, pastors, etc.?" I believe the Lord has "much people"[1] on these campuses; fundamentalists just need to get to work and find them.

Not only does the pastor/manager need to maintain the right relationship with his campus worker and with his fellow pastors supporting the work, but also he also needs to maintain a relationship with the mission board through regular communication. The pastor should be involved in the entire process of selecting a campus pastor/missionary. Cross Impact Ministries can recommend campus missionaries to the local churches; however, there will be times when the pastor already has someone in mind too for this role. In these cases Cross Impact Ministries is willing to further train such a worker and assist if this person needs to be supported on a missionary basis at first. The pastor and Cross Impact Ministries need to work together to establish a support level that fits that local church's financial pay scale for their staff workers. Cross Impact Ministries does not want to see missionaries under-supported, nor does Cross Impact Ministries want to see its missionaries being paid

---

[1] Acts 18:10.

disproportionately as it relates to the salary caps of the local church. For example, it would be unwise for Cross Impact Ministries' missionary to have a support level of $50,000 if the senior pastor is being paid $32,000. Nor would it be appropriate to establish a support level of $18,000 for the missionary if the pastor and his staff are averaging $75,000 a year. The pastor/manager of a campus ministry should regularly evaluate the progress of the campus worker and address any concerns with the missionary first and then, if need be, communicate with Cross Impact Ministries. Cross Impact Ministries does not want to come between the pastor and his college pastor/missionary. All matters of discipline should be conducted at the local-church level. The responsibility of the senior pastor to Cross Impact Ministries is to keep the board informed of any major problems that would relate to the Cross Impact Ministries' name and testimony and of any disciplinary steps taken with a campus pastor/missionary. Also, if the church needs to release the campus pastor/missionary for any reason, the senior pastor should communicate such information to Cross Impact Ministries. It is important for the pastor of the host church to recognize that Cross Impact Ministries has a working relationship not only with him but also with the missionary and his supporting churches. All missionaries are encouraged to maintain their primary loyalty to their Lord, their local church, and their pastor. All of a missionary's concerns should be first directed to his pastor and the leadership of the local church. If the missionary cannot find a biblical resolution, disassociation will take place only after Cross Impact Ministries meets with the pastor to ensure that the missionary has handled his grievances biblically and ethically and that all efforts to reconcile the problems have been exhausted.

For churches using the Cross Impact Ministries name for their campus ministry, the church and Cross Impact Ministries must enter a covenant to maintain the doctrines outlined in the covenant. Such a covenant is signed when the local church desires to have a campus missionary. If the local church drifts from the doctrinal foundation of Cross Impact Ministries, it will be asked to change the name of its campus ministry from Cross Impact Ministries to a name of its choosing. If the campus pastor/missionary agrees with the theological drift of the local church, Cross Impact Ministries will need to release the missionary from Cross Impact Ministries and will notify the supporting churches of the disassociation. Hopefully, such unfortunate disassociations will be minimal. Most of the doctrinal issues can be avoided by careful communication during the initial interviewing process between the pastor and Cross Impact Ministries and the interview process among Cross Impact Ministries, the local pastor, and the missionary. The missionary will go through a doctrinal interview process before even being accepted as a Cross Impact Ministries' missionary. Then he will be interviewed by the pastor of the host church. Such interviews should catch any doctrinal incompatibilities. The pastor/manager of the campus ministry must count the cost of having a campus missionary as it relates to his relationship with the missionary and with the Cross Impact Ministries' mission board.

All of these relationships to be maintained can be viewed as a burden or a blessing by the pastor/manager. The blessings of such relationships are the fellowship, the joy of sharing in a common vision, the additional prayer support, and the healthy accountability.

The obvious downside to so many relationships is the greater likelihood for misunderstandings, strained relationships, and divisions. These issues support the argument for the ultimate goal of each church in a major college town: to have a campus pastor fully supported by the local church. However, in many ways, the advantages of the campus pastor/missionary model far exceed the liabilities. The choice of having a missionary is typically the difference between having a campus ministry or not. Many churches in a college town have thought of having an outreach to the campus for years, but rarely is one successfully started and maintained. Generally the local church relegates the campus ministry to being a ministry that it wishes to have someday. Someday Christians will have to give account for their shortsightedness and negligence in reaching collegians for Christ.

THE PROBLEM OF NOT BEING
ABLE TO MULTIPLY

The sixth problem facing the pastor/manager who has a vision for campus ministry is how he can help the vision of campus ministries spread throughout the state/region and nation. To accomplish this goal, a strategy is being encouraged in this dissertation for each state to follow. The biggest obstacle to campus ministry is funding the position for a full-time campus worker. Humanly speaking, the solution rests upon two sources: local churches within each state funding campus missionaries to reach their own secular campuses within their own state, and then the local church hosting the campus ministry absorbing the full financial burden of their campus pastor. To accomplish this goal there needs to be a mechanism set up to connect the churches in the state with the churches in the college town. This connection can be accomplished by a the statewide/regional aspect of the mission board, such as Cross Impact Ministries or Campus Light Fellowship in West Virginia. Such a mission board must be doctrinally sound and local-church-oriented. The board members should be pastors in the key college towns and solid pastors in the non-college towns. Such a mix will provide good accountability and objectivity. In some of the larger college cities, there might be several churches that are not only near the campus but desirous of a campus ministry. This presents some challenges to the missionary strategy. The options for two churches in the same town interested in campus work are

1. To work together to establish one campus ministry on the campus and direct the students to attend either of the churches. The advantage of this approach is that "two are better than one"[2] when it comes to areas such as student contacts and financial resources to fund a campus missionary. The weakness is that the campus missionary will at times have divided loyalties and more complications to work around with two churches. This approach will make it difficult for the campus pastor/missionary to be on two church staffs. It will also hinder the campus pastor/missionary from being financially absorbed by one local church.

[2]Eccles. 4:9.

2. To work independently and establish two campus ministries on the campus and to direct the students that each group is working with that group's host church. Typically, a large college campus could easily handle two more campus ministries.

3. To establish a campus ministry out of one church, with the other church encouraging and supporting that ministry. The campus pastor/missionary and his host church would be sensitive to the help of the other church and would refer students to that church as well. Typically, students, once saved, will do some "shopping around" and will occasionally find another church more suited to them. To have promoted two good churches in the area is very healthy. The long-term goal could be to divide the campus into two divisions and later to assist the other church in starting a second fundamental campus ministry.

This third option is similar to Cross Impact Ministries' approach for reaching the smaller colleges in the state. The faithful Cross Impact Ministries' worker will be equipped and trained to assist a sister church in a neighboring college town to start a campus ministry. The goal would be to place a campus missionary on all the major campuses and for these ministries to assist other churches in establishing a campus ministry. This can be done by hosting sports outreach events that promote inter-school rivalries, hosting college/career retreats, promoting college/career retreats at The WILDS and other good fundamental camps, etc. Part of the training of the Cross Impact Ministries missionary is to maximize the student's spring break by taking a team of students to another local church in a college town to conduct various evangelistic outreaches on that campus. This promotes the vision for campus ministry and builds a healthy comradeship between the churches. Monthly rallies could be conducted on these neighboring campuses with the aid of the Cross Impact Ministries' missionary. The goal for these smaller colleges would be for the neighboring local church to be trained to reach the students through their own pastoral staff, lay leadership, and, if the need justifies it, a campus pastor/missionary.

The goals to reach one's state/region would be promoted by Cross Impact Ministries at the various pastors' fellowships in the state and in church services where the Cross Impact Ministries missionaries present their burden for campus ministry and the goal to reach not only their appointed campus but also the entire state. One of the most effective ways to promote campus ministries within one's state is to have the state divided into regions and to have the Cross Impact Ministries pastors host a luncheon in each region to present the state goal of reaching collegians for Christ to the pastors in that area. In particular the luncheon organizers would emphasize the goal of providing a campus worker for their regional college(s). These pastors will then be asked to host a deputation meeting with one of the Cross Impact Ministries missionaries. Often in these meetings the missionary will bring students with him who will testify to how they were saved through the campus ministry. These students bring the reality of the need to reach these future leaders with Christ. Also such meetings continue to cultivate the two-way networking of college contacts. Pastors and churches would be encouraged to pray for and to fund the campus missionaries. Monies would be funneled through Cross Impact Ministries and would be used for funding the campus pastor/missionaries. As the local churches hosting the campus ministry absorb the financial responsibility of the campus pastor, the monies freed up would go to other campus pastor/missionary projects. Such revolving funds would facilitate reaching collegians for Christ statewide. Church support of campus missionaries would stay within the state if the missionary resigns or leaves the state to minister elsewhere. Obviously those individuals and churches that want their monies to follow the campus missionary would be welcome to continue that support. However, the goal encouraged by Cross Impact Ministries is for the churches within the state or region (e.g., New England) to maintain the support for the ministries within the state. For example, if a church is supporting a campus missionary at the University of South Carolina and the missionary takes a pastorate in Virginia, Cross Impact Ministries would encourage the supporting churches to maintain the support level for the next missionary at USC.

Ideally the churches within the state/region would support Cross Impact Ministries and the goals to reach the major campuses in the state, and in due time these ministries would "strawberry out" to reach the smaller campuses. The result would be that fundamentalists have a gospel presence on each of the campuses within the state. If this model could be followed successfully in one state, the model could be replicated in other states. The key for expanding into another state will be to find one key pastor/church situated in a college town that is doctrinally and philosophically sound and geared for campus ministry. The search for such a church would begin with the results of the statewide/regional study of the major colleges and the fundamental churches in those towns. Ideally the regional hubs for Cross Impact Ministries would be centrally located, particularly in the west. This is not mandatory, but it can be very beneficial for logistics. Solid pastors in the major college towns and regions would be challenged to start campus ministries and to develop the regional aspects of the board with some other fine pastors from non-college towns. This body would seek to promote the goals as previously discussed. Following the strategy of Cross Impact Ministries in the southeast hub in Clemson, South Carolina, the major campuses within each of the fifty states can eventually have a fundamental campus ministry.

Today the fundamental, Bible-believing churches are ministering to less than one ten-thousandth of one percent of the student population presently enrolled on the state campuses. Fundamentalists as a movement have turned their back on the secular campus. No wonder America is in the state she is in. Christians have neglected to intercept the next generation of leaders with the gospel. What a tragedy; what negligence! One thing is for certain, the state colleges will not instruct the youth to repent of sins and place their trust in the finished work of the Lord Jesus Christ. John Witherspoon, the first president of Princeton, summarized such humanistic learning when he said, "Cursed be all learning that is contrary to the cross of Christ. Cursed be all learning that is not coincident with the cross of Christ. Cursed be all learning that is not subservient to the cross of Christ."[3]

Ironically, colleges that once trained America's pastors and the world's missionaries have now become themselves one of the most needy mission fields in America. Martin Luther said, "I am much

---

[3]Tan, *Illustrations*, 159.

afraid that the universities will prove to be the great gates to Hell, unless they diligently labour to explain the Holy Scriptures and to engrave them upon the hearts of youth. I advise no one to place his child where the Scriptures do not reign paramount. Every institution where men are not unceasingly occupied with the Word of God must become corrupt."[4] Sadly, Luther discerned accurately; colleges have proven to be the great gates to hell. What will fundamentalists do to shut these gates to hell?

---

[4]Ibid.

13

THE CAMPUS PASTOR/
MISSIONARY

While the previous two chapters dealt with the need of pastors and churches to see the vision for campus work, this chapter emphasizes the need of a campus pastor/missionary. It is possible to have too much organizational "string" attached to the kite, and the kite (campus ministry) never gets off the ground. Someone has to get onto the secular campus and present the glorious gospel to students who need salvation.

The greatest need of the hour is campus workers. Christians can philosophize and strategize all they want, but the bottom line is that someone has to go where the students are and preach the gospel. The fundamentalist movement is doctrinally and philosophically strong, but when it comes to actually getting on the campus and winning students to Christ, it is very weak. Fundamentalists criticize the campus parachurch organizations and the compromising new evangelicals, yet they do little to nothing for the souls of collegians. Such hypocrisy cannot please God. Christians need to be "doers of the Word"[1] when it comes to campus ministry. Fundamentalists need to see their neglect for the campuses shift to talk and then to "do."

THE CALL OF THE CAMPUS
PASTOR/MISSIONARY

Tragically, few are being called to campus ministry, primarily because so few are being made aware of the need. As the awareness of

---

[1]James 1:22.

campus ministry increases, there will a corresponding increase in campus workers. The key, therefore, is to make more people aware of the need of campus work.

To increase awareness, fundamentalists need to target pastors and their churches and Bible colleges. If these two groups become aware of the need for campus ministry, people will be burdened to pray, and some people will be called to campus ministry.

However, one of the greatest sources for future workers is the secular campus itself. Students saved and burdened to reach their own generation with the gospel will provide a great working force. As in all ages, the problem is not with the fields that are white unto the harvest but with the shortage of workers. It would not be appropriate to recruit solely from Bible colleges and deplete their resources. Therefore, the goal must be to see secular students saved, trained formally at Bible colleges and informally in local churches, and equipped to serve in any mission field. Some of these will return to minister on the campus, others will go to a foreign field, and some will be godly laymen using their vocation as their mission field. One goal is to develop future workers from those saved on the secular campus. This will increase the work force for God.

THE TRAINING OF THE CAMPUS PASTOR/MISSIONARY

Those who are called to campus work need to be adequately trained, particularly in the Scriptures. The pressure to compromise on the campus is great; therefore, an effective campus ministry demands that the worker be firmly grounded in the Scriptures. He needs to know what he believes and why he believes it, as there is very little time for crystallization of doctrine during the campus ministry. Because the campus worker will be confronted with many theological questions, he must "be ready always to give an answer to every man that asketh you a reason of the hope that is in you with meekness and fear."[2]

---

[2]1Pet. 3:15.

Not only does the campus worker need to carefully define revealed truth, he must also be able to defend its validity. Students are seeking compelling reasons and credible evidence on which to base their faith. Like the apostle Thomas, they want more facts, especially if they are being asked to rely on a source (the Bible) that has been routinely attacked and ridiculed in their classes. They want to be convinced that the Bible is reliable and trustworthy. Therefore, apologetics can prepare the way for evangelism on the campus, in which the Holy Spirit convicts the students as they hear the simple gospel message being preached.

The campus pastor/missionary must have the theological background to be able to contend, confound, dispute, persuade, reason, warn, exhort, and "convince the gainsayers."[3] By the use of sound doctrine, the campus worker must be able to refute error and stop the mouths of those who are subverting others from the truth. Therefore, the campus worker must have a strong background in Bible and theology.

If any ministry puts a premium on education, it is the secular college ministry. The Catholics, the cults, and some of the new evangelical groups have highly trained staff workers ministering to the students. The fundamentalists should have no less as the strength of the campus ministry must be sound doctrine. Therefore, although there is a place for undergraduate Bible students on campus extension ministries and campus internships, a full-time campus worker generally should have a master's degree in a Bible-related field or be actively pursuing such a degree. Programs such as the master of divinity and doctor of ministry are very well suited to campus pastors and their schedules.

Most fundamental Bible colleges will provide the campus worker with a strong theological foundation, especially if he pursues a seminary degree (e.g., master of divinity). Sadly, however, the Bible college student will receive little to no practical training related to campus ministry as part of his formal program. The result of this oversight is that fundamentalists are neglecting the mission field of

---

[3]Titus 1:9.

the secular campus and doing a very shabby job ministering to the college/career members of their churches. One of the greatest needs in Bible college curriculums is for a course that provides training for campus ministry. This course would give the Bible college student the practical tools needed to "serve his own generation"[4] on the secular college campus. Such a class on campus evangelism would also raise the awareness for campus ministry and would assist in bringing more workers to the campus.

Along with the Bible colleges becoming aware and alert to the need of reaching collegians for Christ, pastors also need to see the need and get a burden for reaching the students. If the pastors and the churches do not have a burden for such a ministry, the campus missionary's efforts will be greatly hindered. The need then is for pastors, churches, and Bible colleges to be made aware of the need for taking the gospel to the campus. As this awareness grows, formal and practical training needs to be put in place so that those who are called to campus ministry will be readily and properly equipped to tackle these fortresses of infidelity.

An existing training method is for Bible college students to go on extension to a college campus with an established campus ministry. This provides opportunities for witnessing, leading small group Bible studies, distributing tracts, getting involved in activities, and participating in sports outreaches. This exposure to the campus will only increase the student's burden for reaching the lost, in particular the secular college student. As a prerequisite, the extension worker would attend a special training meeting that would prepare him for ministering in the culture of a secular college campus. Included in this training should be an overview of the soulwinning and discipleship materials that the church recommends and has available. Such one-day training sessions should be offered at the start of the fall and spring semesters. Because each campus has its own set of rules and guidelines, violations of which can jeopardize the campus ministry's charter, extension workers need to be properly trained so that they don't do more harm than good on the campus.

---

[4]Acts 13:36.

Another training opportunity is the regional training conference for potential campus workers, pastors, and laymen. This conference also provides active campus workers with fellowship and encouragement. Hosted by a regional hub which would include the host pastor, the campus worker(s) and the local church, the conference includes preaching for the entire church family during the evenings of the conference. During the day there are seminars dealing with the "nuts and bolts" of campus ministry as well as real opportunities to observe some major aspect of campus ministry (i.e. international day, a sports outreach tournament, etc.).

A step beyond these training opportunities would be a class on secular campus evangelism offered at a Bible college. Such a class, whether a block class, a video class, or a traditional class, would offer the student a comprehensive study on the topic and would provide the best academic preparation for the campus ministry. This class could also address the need of developing an effective college/career ministry within the local church, which would broaden the class so that it applied to practically every local church in the country, regardless of whether a college is close by. As long as the church had college/career-aged students, this class would equip the local church in ministering to them.

Beyond the classroom training, an internship would allow the interested campus worker to receive the theory of campus ministry and practical hands-on training on the campus. Such an internship can take a variety of formats. For example, during a summer internship the interested worker would work underneath a campus pastor/missionary and assist in the work. This type of internship is particularly useful for those who are still in school and are looking for a unique summer ministry. In addition, some Bible colleges might give college credit for such an internship if it met defined requirements. In some cases the intern's summer schedule may correspond with the summer sessions of the secular university so that the Bible student could take a class at the secular school and be thrust immediately into the mainstream of the student population. This "Gospel Horse" approach brings the summer intern into immediate contact with his peers and lends itself to numerous witnessing opportunities. An intern could also help with a summer mission team that is assisting a local church in starting its own campus ministry.

The other internship option is for the interested worker to train under a campus pastor/missionary for a minimum of one year. The intern would be a great help to the established campus pastor/missionary, and the established worker would be a great help to the intern. After the training period the intern would seek the Lord as to what church to work with to pioneer a campus ministry. With so few fundamental campus ministries in America, it would not be difficult for him to find a campus at which to pioneer a work.

THE NEED OF WOMEN CAMPUS WORKERS

There is a great need for single ladies to assist with the campus ministry. As noted earlier, sixty percent of the students enrolled in America are females. A lady can conduct Bible studies in the girls' dorm rooms and is able to minister to the female students in ways that a male campus worker cannot. However, the wife of the campus worker typically has limited involvement on the campus because of her calling to minister to her husband and children. She often does not have time to get on campus to minister to the many needs of the female college student. Therefore, any campus ministry would be greatly helped by having a single lady as a campus staff worker. The church would need to develop clear guidelines for her role in the overall ministry at church and on the campus. There must also be a healthy trust and relationship between her and the college pastor's wife.

THE PROCESS OF BECOMING A CAMPUS PASTOR/MISSIONARY

If someone believes he is being called to campus ministries, he should share this information with his family and home church first. Pastors want to hear of such great news firsthand and not through the grapevine. Also, pastors strongly desire to be in the initial planning stages of ministry instead of after-the-fact encounters. The person called to campus ministry should discuss and evaluate the various approaches and philosophies to campus ministry with his pastor. Some pastors may simply recommend the missionary model, while others may strongly state that the campus pastor/missionary model articulated in this dissertation is the best approach. Regardless, the pastor and the one called to the campus should agree on the best approach. The campus missionary is best served when his home church and pastor back the missionary project.

The next step is to seek the Lord as to which church to work with and which campus to minister to. There will be times when a campus missionary will have a burden for a particular secular campus but will be unable to find a good fundamental church to work from. Such a college town would be an excellent place to plant a church and then start a campus ministry. In other cases a good church may be found, but the local church may not have the burden for reaching collegians for Christ. Some churches are intimidated by the prospect of a campus ministry, while others may not want to invest their resources in such a transient segment of their community or may not want to minister to those who are culturally different. The key for the campus pastor/missionary is to find a doctrinally sound church that is balanced and has a heart for people and outreach. After finding such a church, the campus pastor/missionary should set up an appointment with the pastor of that local church. They should discuss the vision and agree on their philosophy for campus ministry. Some churches have the financial wherewithal to fully fund the office of the campus pastor, a fact that makes planning much easier. However, if the church is not in a position to fully fund the office, the worker must take a part-time job, go on deputation as a missionary, or a combination of both. As presented in this dissertation, the pastor, church, and campus worker should have a shared long-term goal for the local church to fully absorb the financial responsibilities of the campus worker. A good campus worker will ultimately bring in enough families to more than bear that burden and will therefore basically pay for himself.

If the worker needs missionary support or feels called to campus ministry but is not sure where to minister, he will need to prayerfully seek the Lord as to what mission board to serve with. An interview should be set up with the mission board representative, at which ministry goals should be discussed. If the Lord leads the worker to join a mission board, the worker will normally have to complete an application and formal interview process. The full-time campus worker should meet all of the scriptural requirements of the pastor and should be recognized as a God-called, ordained minister of the gospel. He should not serve as a deacon in the local church while serving as a campus pastor. He has been called to ministry and uniquely equipped to minister the Word of God.

Pastors who have a vision for reaching their local secular campus and who seek initial assistance from a mission board should work hand in hand with the board in recruiting a campus worker. It is ideal for the pastor to be involved in the process of selecting a campus missionary from the beginning. There will be times when the pastor may already have in mind a campus worker who may need only some hands-on training and some prodding to consider praying about being a campus missionary.

The earlier the pastor and church are involved in the recruitment process and the more ownership of the project that they take, the better. One of the largest complaints of campus missionaries is the lack of local church support, involvement, and ownership. The success of the campus ministry will depend on the amount of the pastor's and church's involvement with the campus pastor/missionary. If the local church just wants a worker on the campus, the campus ministry will flounder, and when the missionary leaves, the campus work will cease. Therefore, the more the campus ministry can be integrated into the local church family, the greater the likelihood of having a successful ministry.

DEPUTATION FOR THE CAMPUS MISSIONARY

Deputation for the campus worker is greatly enhanced when the missionary's home church and the church where he will minister are strongly behind the project. The church that benefits from the campus worker should give a substantial amount of financial support as early as possible. As discussed in previous chapters, the goal should be for the church to fully absorb the financial responsibilities of the campus pastor/missionary within a few years. The best approach for deputation is to present the vision for campus work to the pastors within the state at luncheons or conferences. If the pastors within the state catch the vision, the campus missionary's deputation will be greatly facilitated. Without strong support from the missionary's home church and ministry-based church and without a statewide vision shared by pastors within the state, the campus missionary will have a very difficult time raising support for the campus ministry. This is not to discourage those campus missionaries, but it does highlight the reality of a flawed deputation system, especially for home mission projects and the campus work. Unfortunately, a church in West Virginia will share little of a burden for a campus ministry in Vermont. However, a church in West Virginia will likely be more interested in supporting a campus ministry at West Virginia University. Placing more of the burden on the local churches within the state and region will make deputation much easier and will facilitate scheduling of update meetings at supporting churches.

Attractive prayer cards and an appealing slide presentation will be helpful tools for the campus missionary on deputation. Most churches do not have a good feel for what is involved in campus ministry. Also, many people in local churches do not know of the doctrinal deficiencies of Campus Crusade, Navigators, InterVarsity, and other campus organizations and will wonder why another campus ministry is needed and why they can't just support those already on the campus. Another minefield that the campus missionary will face on deputation is the issue of what Bible version he or the students use. It is hard for many people in fundamental churches to understand how biblically illiterate secular students are and how rare it is for any of them to have a Bible of any version. Some churches will not allow any time for campus workers to instruct secular students about Bible translations or will not tolerate the worker's using a Bible version other than the King James Version (KJV). This attitude can be very frustrating, especially if the campus worker has a ministry with international students who already have a difficult time understanding modern English. For most international students, the Elizabethan English of the KJV presents another barrier to understanding truth.

Deputation for any type of missionary is difficult, but the campus missionary will face many challenges while raising support for a ministry that is not understood. During deputation the campus missionary needs to reinforce the international nature of campus ministry and the importance of the local churches within that state seeing their responsibility to reach their own students.

CONCLUSION

Indeed campus ministry contains many challenges, but along with each challenge, difficulty, and setback are innumerable blessings. The greatest blessing of all is to know that one is fulfilling the Great Commission and pleasing the Lord Jesus Christ. Secular college students fit the scope of ministry as presented in the Great Commission. Therefore Christians cannot choose to ignore or neglect such a mission field without serious repercussions. These repercussions are America's future and the eternal destiny of college students. Today's college student will be tomorrow's leader. In the 1990s America saw the fruit of those who attended college during the 1960s. The college years give the local church an incredible opportunity to reach students who are strategically consolidated and are genuinely searching for answers to life's questions. Their college days are the link between their parent's home and establishing their own home. It is a time when the student is choosing a vocation, a spouse, and a philosophy for living. Once the students scatter after graduation, they are welded to the mainstream of society and will be tough to find and reach. Therefore, their college years are the crossroads at which Christians need to meet them with the truth. Luther accurately stated that universities are "the great gates to hell." There is no better time for reaching those who were not reached with the gospel as children or young teens than during their college years. Who is going to serve this generation? What will be the fundamentalists' motto for reaching collegians in the twenty-first century? Will it be "Taking the Cross of Christ to the Campus"?

Who will pray that the Lord of the harvest would send forth laborers into the field of campus ministry? The secular campus needs workers who will pray for the campus, who will be so overwhelmed with the burden that they will be constrained by the Spirit of God and the love of Christ to reach collegians for Christ. Who would be willing to be such an ambassador for Christ on the secular college campus?

In the quad of fraternity houses at Clemson University, there is one "frat house" from which Shannon Gill fell twenty-seven feet to her death. Shannon was drunk, having been served alcohol at a local bar as well as at the fraternity house, despite her being under the legal drinking age. The night of her death, she climbed out of a window and was climbing the ledge to another room on the third floor. In the process, she stumbled and fell. Her parents lost their precious daughter and filed a lawsuit against the bar and the fraternity. Approximately a year later, an article in the *Greenville News* read, "Fraternity, bar cleared in student's fatal fall." Will Christians at the judgment seat of Christ be cleared of the "students' fatal fall" in America?

Selected Bibliography

Books and Pamphlets

Adams, Jay. *Competent to Counsel*. Grand Rapids: Zondervan, 1970.

———. *The Christian Counselor's Manual*. Grand Rapids: Baker, 1973.

Alexander, Archibald. *The Log College: Biographical Sketches of William Tennent and His Students*. London: Banner of Truth, 1968.

Anderson, Courtney. *To the Golden Shore*. Valley Forge, PA: Judson Press, 1987.

Beale, David. *The Mayflower Pilgrims*. Greenville, SC: Ambassador-Emerald International, 2000.

Berg, James A. *Basics for Believers*. Greenville, SC: Bob Jones University Press, 1978.

———. *Changed Into His Image*. Greenville, SC: BJU Press, 1999.

Bright, Bill. *Come Help Change the World*. Old Tappan, NJ: Revell, 1970.

Budziszewski, J. *How to Stay Christian in College*. Colorado Springs: NavPress, 1971.

Curtis, A. Kenneth, Stephen J. Lang, and Randy Petersen. *The 100 Most Important Events in Christian History*. Grand Rapids: Revell, 1991.

Dallimore, Arnold. *George Whitefield: Volumes 1 and 2*. Carlisle, PA: Banner of Truth, 1979, 1980.

———. *A Heart Set Free*. London: Evangelical Press, 1988.

———. *Spurgeon*. Chicago: Moody Press, 1984.

D'Aubigné, Jean Henri Merle. *The Triumph of Truth*. Greenville, SC: Bob Jones University Press, 1996.

Dunn, Charles W. *Campus Crusade—Its Message and Methods*. Greenville, SC: Bob Jones University Press, 1990.

Edwards, Jonathan. *A Treatise on Religious Affections*. Grand Rapids: Baker, 1982.

Fremont, Trudy and Walter. *Becoming an Effective Christian Counselor*. Greenville, SC: Bob Jones University Press, 1996.

Grubb, Norman. *C. T. Studd: Cricketer and Pioneer*. Fort Washington, PA: Christian Literature Crusade, 1982.

Hamrick, Frank. *Ancient Landmarks: A Guide to Personal Standards*. Rocky Mount, NC: Positive Action for Christ, 1980.

———. *Bread*. Rocky Mount, NC: Positive Action for Christ, 1977.

Hodge, Charles. *Princeton Sermons*. Carlisle, PA: Banner of Truth, 1979.

Kearns, Richard A. *Directive Discipleship: Winning Others and Training Others to Win*. Greenville, SC: The Forever Generation, 1977.

Kershaw, Max. *How to Share the Good News with Your International Friend*. Colorado Springs: International Students Inc., 1990.

Lacock, Melvin T. *Won by One Bible Study Course*. Des Moines: Bible Press Inc., 1987.

Latourette, Kenneth Scott. *A Short History of the Far East*. New York: Macmillan, 1968.

Lawrence, Carl. *The Church in China*. Minneapolis: Bethany, 1985.

Lehman, Mark. *Joy Abounding*. Taichung, Taiwan: Beachhead to a Billion, 1999.

Mack, Wayne. *A Homework Manual for Biblical Living: Volume 1*. Phillipsburg, NJ: Presbyterian & Reformed Publishing, 1979.

Miller, Hal. *Campus Bible Fellowship Staff Manual.* Cleveland: Baptist Mid-Missions Publishing, 1977.

Moody, Dwight Lyman. *College Students at Northfield.* New York: Revell, 1888.

Morrison, Peter. *Making Friends with Mainland Chinese Students.* Robesonia, PA: Christian Communications Ltd., 1986.

Muller, George. *The Autobiography of George Muller.* Springdale, PA: Whitaker House, 1984.

Murray, Iain H. *Revival and Revivalism: The Making and Marring of American Evangelicalism.* Carlisle, PA: Banner of Truth, 1994.

Nelson, Ed. *Growing in Grace.* Denver: Mile-Hi Publishers, 1991.

———. *My Morning Manna.* Denver: Mile-Hi Publishers, 1990.

Nelson, Ethel R., and Richard E. Broadberry. *God's Promise to the Chinese.* Dunlap, TN: Read Books, 1997.

New Topical Memory System. Colorado Springs: The Navigators, 1969.

Piggin, Stuart, and John Roxborogh. *The St. Andrews Seven.* Carlisle, PA: Banner of Truth, 1985.

Real Life Ministries Pictorial Review. Greenville, SC: Real Life Ministries, 1984.

Senn, William J., III. *The Ploughman's Harvest Series.* Westminster, CO: Cross Impact Press, 2003.

———. *The Ploughman's Journal.* Westminster, CO: Cross Impact Press, 2003.

———. *The Ploughman's Manual.* Westminster, CO: Cross Impact Press, 2003.

———. *The Ploughman's Sower Series.* Westminster, CO: Cross Impact Press, 2003.

———. *Sports Outreaches.* Westminster, CO: Cross Impact Press, 2003.

Sidwell, Mark. *Faith of our Fathers: Scenes from American Church History.* Greenville, SC: Bob Jones University Press, 1991.

Skinner, Betty Lee. *DAWS*. Grand Rapids: Zondervan, 1974.

Terrill, Ross. *800,000,000: The Real China*. Boston: Atlantic-Little, Brown, 1972.

Trotman, Dawson. *Born to Reproduce*. Lincoln, NE: Back to the Bible, 1978.

Van Halsema, Thea B. *Three Men Came to Heidelberg and Glorious Heretic*. Grand Rapids: Baker, 1991.

Walton, Robert, C. *Chronological and Background Charts of Church History*. Grand Rapids: Zondervan, 1986.

Wang, Samuel, and Ethel R. Nelson. *God and the Ancient Chinese*. Dunlap, TN: Read Books, 1998.

Wei, Christian. *A Bilingual University in Mainland China*. Greenville, SC: Christian Wei Missions, 1997.

Wheeler, Tom. *What You Should Know About the Church of Christ*. Taylors, SC: Real Life Ministries, 1980.

Wood, Skevington. *The Burning Heart*. Minneapolis: Bethany Fellowship Inc., 1967.

Woodbridge, Charles. *Campus Crusade Examined in the Light of Scripture*. Greenville, SC: Bob Jones University Press, 1970.

Woods, C. Stacey. *The Growth of a Work of God*. Downers Grove, IL: InterVarsity Press, 1978.

Xinhua, Lu. *The Wounded: New Stories of the Cultural Revolution 77–78*. Hong Kong: Joint Publishing Co., 1979.

PERIODICALS

Austin, Alvyn. "Missions Dream Team." *Christian History*, November 1996, 19–23.

Dollar, George W. "Campus Crusade and Their Four Spiritual Laws." *Faith for the Family*, May/June 1975, 3.

Koerner, Brendan I. "A New Gender Gap: Where the Boys Aren't." *U.S. News and World Report*, February 8, 1999, 49–55.

Lieber, Ron, Carolyn Kleiner, and Joellen Perry. "2000 Annual

Guide: Best Graduate Schools." *U.S. News and World Report*, March 29, 1999, 74–115.

Ray, James, "Aldergate Street." *BIMI Europe*, April 2001, 3–6.

Roche, George. "How Government Funding is Destroying American Higher Education." *Imprimis,* October 1994, 10.

Stultz, Tom. "Salt-Free Campuses." *Faith for the Family*, November 1980, 8.

Wright, Rusty. "In the Shadow of the '60s." *Moody*, November 1991, 80–85.

Dissertations

Bledsoe, Paul E. "Making Disciples of University Students." Master of Ministry field project, Cincinnati Christian Seminary, 1986.

Duncan, Daniel D. "Community Colleges: Methodology for Developing Ongoing Campus Ministries." Master of Christian Ministries thesis, International School of Theology, 1989.

Kong, Mee Lin. "A Biblical Approach to Chinese Campus Ministry." Master of Arts thesis, Calvary Theological Seminary, 1994.

Loescher, Walter O. "An Analysis of the Anthropological and Soteriological Conflicts in the Theology of Timothy Dwight and his Influence on Nathaniel William Taylor and New Haven Theology." PhD dissertation, Bob Jones University, 1993.

Miles, Lee Ewing. "An Analysis of the Decline of the Influence of the Church in Higher Education." PhD dissertation, Bob Jones University, 1958.

Mitchel, Dennis W. "A Disciple-Making Manual for the Secularized Campus." Master of Arts dissertation, Dallas Theological Seminary, 1984.

Wei, Christian. "The Analysis and Criticism of the Theology and Methodology of Paul Yonggi Cho." PhD dissertation, Bob Jones University, 1992.